SKAGIT RIVER ANTHOLOGY

PRODUCED BY

SKAGIT VALLEY WRITERS LEAGUE

Skagit
Valley
Writers
League

SKAGIT RIVER ANTHOLOGY

For Aspiring Authors New and Old

FOREWORD

Robert Mottram

2021

Welcome to the *Skagit River Anthology,* produced by the Skagit Valley Writers League. Between these covers lies a treasure put here for you by people who share a common obsession. They are writers, and writers write because they must, because they are people driven by an urgent need to share their thoughts on paper or on a digital screen.

The Skagit Valley Writers League is a northwest Washington organization that has drawn creative people together for more than six decades. They gather in search of inspiration, encouragement and friendship, and they cover a wide spectrum. Some seek to sell their first articles or poems or perhaps even their first book. Most, however, already are publishing veterans. Some, in fact, have written books that sell hundreds of thousands of copies. As members of the Writers League, these people come together not as competitors but as colleagues, to share hard-won professional skills and to boost each other's opportunities for success.

The title of this book celebrates the river that dramatically impacts the culture of the place where most of our writers live, lovely northwest Washington. The title also serves as a metaphor that speaks to the quality of the writers whose work appears here. The Skagit is not widely known outside of Washington state despite the fact it is the third-largest river on the entire west coast of the lower 48. It is the only one in that entire area that produces viable populations of all five of the species of Pacific Salmon that are indigenous to North America, and it is the major contributor of salmon to Washington's iconic Puget Sound.

The Skagit rises in the mountains of southwest British Columbia, quickly crosses into Washington, and races westward through the Skagit Valley to the Salish Sea, about 150 miles from its source. En route, it drains about 1.7 million acres of Washington and British Columbia, carrying vast quantities of soil and other organic matter downstream every year. This is yet another reason that people who know the Skagit value it so greatly. The river deposits, on the broad plain it crosses just before entering the sea, much of the material it carries, and has created – mile for mile and over millennia – one of the most productive agricultural areas on the planet. Count that as yet another local secret.

Likewise, though some of the writers found on these pages are not widely known outside their Pacific Northwest environment, their quality, like that of their beloved river, is considered first rate by people familiar with their work.

Since its creation in 1958, the Skagit Valley Writers League has produced an anthology every few years, to give its members yet another opportunity to display their work, and to provide readers with an opportunity to access it. This year, the effort was organized as a contest, in three categories: short story, creative nonfiction, and poetry. Each of the entries is contained in this anthology. Sixteen of the League's writers entered 25 pieces of work.
Contest winners are:

Short Stories
First, *Day of Reckoning* by Craig Martelle
Second, *An Extraordinary Creche* by Darlene Dubay
Third, *Alaska Yukon Pacific Exposition* by Naomi Wark
Honorable Mention, *The Missing Moon* by Gloria Two-Feathers

Nonfiction
First, *Existing in a Time of Pandemic* by Ann Bodle-Nash
Second, *The Purple-Maroon Gym Suit* by Mary Ann Schradi
Third, *The French Doll* by Bruce Lawson
Honorable Mention, *The Capuhtiller* by Kim Kimmy

Poetry
First, *Bootstraps* by Deborah Magnuson
Second, *Sons of the Wind* by Gloria Two-Feathers
Third, *Quicksand* by Sully
Honorable Mention, *Owls Circle* by Mary Ann Schradi, *Moving Moon* by Kathleen Kaska,

What is in a Name by Gloria Two-Feathers

We are happy you have chosen to visit the pages of our 2021 anthology. We hope and we trust that you will find here the kind of entertaining and thought-provoking work that will make you glad you risked your time with us.

Contents

Craig Martelle

DAY OF RECKONING

They said we had real problems. They said they knew what they were doing.

A shadow passing through the great square of Pegasus as seen at the Keck Observatory in Hawaii. Possible comet.

If only that would have made the news instead of what was showing.

"Who cares!" Dad roared at the screen. Mom glared, not at the television but at him. He caught her look and threw his hands up. He seized the remote and changed the channel until he found a comedy. He put the remote down, his gaze challenging her.

"It's important to watch the news, dear," she said, making no attempt to engage in a battle for channel dominance. "You think it doesn't affect us, but it does. It's better to be in the know, don't you think, even if it's just knowing what the topic is."

"Doesn't affect us." Dad vigorously shook his head. "They're telling us it does, but it doesn't. Why aren't they talking about real issues, stuff like higher prices? The news is a glorified gossip show. Who said what about whom. Bah! I don't need that. We're in control because we can change the channel."

I was good with it. We had one computer for the family and no one could use it after dinner. That was supposed to be our family time. We usually watched television like three zombies.

"We're taking the dog for a walk." Mom stood and tipped her chin at me as she did when she had a secret that she wasn't sharing with the old man. I was more than happy to go outside. This episode was a rerun.

New comet alert! 18th magnitude blip. Astronomer names it Vidar.

As soon as Mom grabbed the leash off the hook, our big Golden Retriever ran down the hallway, slipping and sliding on the hardwood. It was always the same. Out of control with overwhelming joy. Dad turned off the television and stood. Mom smiled.

"I'll come, too, if you don't mind. The world is out there, not in here. I need to restore my faith in humanity."

We trooped outside, with Dad taking the leash as he was big enough to hold the dog back whenever he saw a squirrel and tried to chase it.

The neighborhood was a mishmash of humanity. Some were old and barely left their homes. Others had teenagers. I knew all of them because we went to school together. Some had small children, but not many. The younger people moved farther away from the city and suffered the commute.

"Guano face!" Billy May called from his yard, where his Mom loomed over him while he weeded the shrubs. He'd been dodging it for a week. She must have cornered him at dinner.

"Fecal face," I called back, waving, earning myself one of Mom's patented glares. Dad taught me the only defense was to ignore it until she gave up. I mumbled an apology without making eye contact.

An old neighborhood with older houses and plenty of room in between. It was in the city. Richer people moved to the burbs. At least Dad had a short commute to work and back, a job where he'd been in the same position for fifteen years. He never talked about work anymore. He had nothing left to say about it.

Our walk covered two miles. Mom and Dad said it stretched the legs. I didn't get much stretching. The dog didn't walk that fast. He had to sniff everything and deliver a golden sprinkle to those markers he considered worthy.

Comet Vidar slowing due to unidentified gravitic interference suggesting a micro-sized black hole. NASA steering the Startreader probe closer to gather more data.

School wound down as we approached summer break. Collectively, the teachers and students surrendered to the inevitability of it all. They gave us a bunch of tests. We took them. We packed up our lockers and left the school. I doubted the teachers even graded those tests. I was fine with that. I'd done good enough, learning what I needed to know to start next year, if only I'd remember it come fall.

Probably not, but I'd relearn it quickly enough when the time came. Now was my time to forget everything.

Summer vacation. We were driving to Florida for a week at Disney World. It was where princesses could be found. I couldn't wait.

"How long until we leave?" I asked that very day, the last day of school.

"I'm not too sure," Dad said. "We have to tighten our belts a little. Gas and groceries are digging into our vacation money."

The assault on my summer plans hit me between the eyes like a cannonball. When I recovered, I found Dad watching me. "Maybe I could cut grass for people. Weed their shrubs. Would that help?"

"It would. That's very adult of you. Your Mother is looking for a job, too. A few extra nickels would go a long way to filling the coffers."

I didn't know what he meant, except that my vacation was on the line. It was the ultimate call to action. I took out the mower, cleaned it, filled it with the last of our gas, and rolled it down the street, stopping by each yard that could use a trim.

We weren't the only family watching our pennies. But old Mrs. Johnson was kind and asked if I'd take ten dollars to cut her grass. I agreed immediately despite the size of her yard. It took me an hour and I burned most of my tank of gas. I used her rake to collect the piles and bagged them using her bags. I left the tidy refuse along the side of her garage. I saw she had a gas can that looked full.

I wanted to refill my tank, but Dad wouldn't take it kindly if anyone accused me of stealing. I knocked on the door to tell her I was done.

She answered and handed over a ten-dollar bill.

"I used my full tank of gas," I started. I felt bad because I had implied the gas was on me. "I didn't think it would, but it did. Would it be okay if I refilled the tank from your can?"

She laughed until she coughed. "Your labor is worth the money. I don't need you to pay for the gas, too. Of course, and then if you'd held me further, take the can to the station and refill it for me." She handed me a twenty.

I stared at it. I had never gotten gas before and wasn't sure how to do it.

She could see from the look on my face. The older one got, the wiser they seemed to be. "Just see the young lady behind the counter, and she'll turn the pump on for you. Be careful a car doesn't run you over."

She seemed to be able to read minds. "I'll be right back." I ran to the shed, grabbed the can without slowing down and almost yanked my arm from the socket. It was mostly full. I hoped she wasn't watching as I returned and filled my mower before heading out again.

Filling it was as she suggested. Easy and quick. Carrying a full gas can back to her house was a little more work than I expected, but it was my first paying job, and I had done it all by myself. I dropped the can off in the back, rinsed my hands with a garden hose, dried them on my shirt, and returned to the house where I handed over the change. Twelve dollars' worth. I would have only made two dollars had I not asked.

Business. I had gotten lucky. This time.

"Keep the change." She smiled with heavily wrinkled eyes, the good scars of age. "Every Saturday morning, after eight because I sleep in, I would like you to cut my lawn. Ten dollars plus gas. Deal?" We shook on it. She seemed more like a grandmother, one who would hug me mercilessly.

I was happy she didn't.

Vidar classified as rogue meteor. Now 12th magnitude brightness.

Mom couldn't find a job, and then Dad got laid off. Vacation was canceled. I realized that I was too busy. My client list was growing. Some of the houses were a long way away, friends of Mrs. Johnson's. At least they let me use their mowers so I could ride my bike to the job. It took me all day Saturday and all day Sunday to get the jobs done. I'd take Monday and Tuesday to rest and then back at it Wednesday through Friday for those people who wanted their yards looking nice for the weekend as opposed to *doing* the cutting and trimming on the weekend.

It wasn't long before I had as much work as I could do. People complimented me on my strong work ethic. It was tiring.

At dinner one evening, my Dad sat with his head hanging low. "I'm sorry," he muttered. Mom put a few slices of fried bologna on the table and a salad made of dandelion greens with olive oil on the side. There was one potato that Mom had cut into three parts.

"I don't understand." I didn't. I liked fried bologna.

Asking seemed like the easiest way to get to the bottom of the problem. Mom had taught me that. If you're lost, ask for directions, something my Dad would never do.

"We don't have enough money to buy decent food. We won't make our mortgage payment this month either."

Money.

"Damn, Dad!" Mother shook her finger at me. "I mean, I've turned down some jobs because there's only one of me. If you help me, I can take those and we can get it all done. Just a man helping his son. Wait a minute."

I went to my room to get two things. A lockbox I had found in the trash and a coin bank bust of George Washington.

"Here. Take it all. It was for vacation, but I'm too busy to take time off." I laughed and put my hand over my Mom's. She was crying. That told me I'd done the right thing. Dad was never happy when Mom cried, but today was different.

Everything was different.

He looked up and smiled. "Are you offering me a job? And telling me it comes with a signing bonus?"

I thought it was simpler than that. We were one family. But if Dad needed those terms to internalize it, then yes. "I am."

"Take this to the bank tomorrow and let's set our checking account right." He pushed the money toward Mom. "The men of this family will be at work."

And that's what it became. We cut grass and then we started trimming bushes along with other yard work. We even expanded into other outdoor activities like scraping paint, which I didn't care much for so we charged more. People seemed okay with paying it. We lost clients and gained clients while we continued to grow.

Dad and I kept the family afloat. "Do it with a smile," Dad said. "People don't like being around grumpy people. I learned that the hard way. I made it easy for them to let me go, and I didn't even realize it. We may not be making enough to go on vacation, but we're surviving. That is the most important lesson of all. Come fall, we'll figure it out. Maybe your Mom can fill in for you while you're at school."

"Mom?"

"We'll do what we have to." Dad was trying to be reassuring, but he sounded confident.

Mom still hadn't been able to find a real job either, although I was learning that 'real' was relative. I worked hard. I couldn't remember the last time I watched television. I hated to take money out of my earnings for new shoes, but I'd worn mine out. Dad took me to the good store where he bought his last pair of work boots. We bought mine a little big so I'd get more use out of them. He figured I was still growing. He knew that I'd keep working.

Vidar heading toward Earth.

We finished early one evening and Dad held his nose while turning on the news. It had been a while.

"Vidar?" Dad wondered why the talking heads spent an hour arguing about two minutes worth of facts. No one knew anything besides they thought it was a comet, then it was an asteroid, and now it was something different. NASA didn't say it, but the gossip group couldn't say the word enough.

Aliens.

"Get out," Dad scoffed. He made to change the channel, but Mom wanted to watch.

"What are they doing about it? Where's the government?"

"Can I get on the computer?" I didn't think the people on television had the answer. They seemed almost apoplectic despite the calls from officials to remain calm.

Neither Mom nor Dad answered so I took that as a 'yes.' Online, I searched through too many pages that were more commentary.

No one knew anything. I had one simple question. What about us?

I turned the computer off and returned to the living room where Mom and Dad were having a spirited debate with the on-screen personalities who rehashed the same points. My parents were taking exception to everything. I stood in front of the television. They tried to look around me but only briefly until they realized I wasn't going to move.

"How does this affect us?" I wanted to know.

Dad looked at my Mom and she shook her head. She talked to my Dad. "You started this months ago when you asked that same question. Before the economy tanked."

Mom said it that way rather than saying Dad lost his job. Dad had tried to explain that ten percent unemployment didn't count those who stopped looking for work. He figured one out of four were out of work but that meant three out of four were working, and that's who we worked for. We worked twice as hard, twice as long hours to cover what Dad had previously made.

It allowed me to get a new pair of boots. We had eaten a lot of hot dogs that summer because we were saving for a rainy day. We upgraded to hamburgers on special days. Both with day old buns but the steamer took care of that. Hot dogs on steamed buns. It was like every day was a trip to the ballpark

"Looking to the government for answers is like asking the dog to take out the trash."

I looked at Mom. She shrugged.

"So, no answers?" I guessed.

"No. All the credit, none of the blame, and no direction."

Dad had grown bitter after losing his job, but lightened up through the summer. We had a lot of fun while working hard. Dad always made sure that I collected the money. He told my clients that he worked for me.

He was my best employee. Better than me because he knew why the grass grew or didn't. I only cut it. We made a good team.

"Do we keep working?"

My Dad smiled. "Will the grass keep growing?"

I nodded.

"If they are aliens, maybe they'll appreciate us more if we put a good face on the neighborhood. If they stopped here, how would you feel if the yards weren't in their best shape?"

I shook my head. I took my job seriously.

"What do you say we do one bonus yard each day, for free, just to make sure everyone looks as good as they can."

That was something I could get behind, but wasn't sure where we'd find the time. He gestured toward Mom. He knew that we were topped out. I had to laugh.

That made her mad but she didn't stay angry for long. "Just wait and see." And then she disappeared into the kitchen to make cookies for us.

I was always up for a bribe. I was the boss, after all.

Arrival. Alien spacecraft in orbit over Earth. Pandemonium.

It was all anyone could talk about. Four houses were unable to pay us because the banks had run out of cash. Dad suggested we collect our pay in food. They agreed even though food prices were going up with what people called Armageddon. I had thought that was a movie.

It was, so we watched it to see what the big deal was.

The end of days. But at the hands of an asteroid not aliens.

"Nothing has changed," I argued.

My Dad was confused. "Everything has changed. Our fundamental understanding of the universe is now different. We are not alone."

"But how does that affect us?" We had a full pantry and cupboards for the first time since Dad lost his job. I felt pretty good but didn't understand the cognitive dissonance coming from those who were supposed to be in charge.

And that gave their critics fits.

No one had a way ahead. Wait. Attack. Reach out. Shore up defenses. No one knew, but everyone had an opinion. Not me. I had grass to cut.

Dad and I went out each morning and did our job. When we reached the point where half of our clients were unable to pay and unable to trade anything, it did us in. We couldn't afford the gas to do the jobs, even if we accepted IOUs, the gas station did not.

So, we worked until we ran out of gas and called it a day. Dad insisted on visiting every home and telling them. We found two that were able to pay, so we rolled our dry mower to their houses, asked to be paid in advance for the day's work, while Dad physically ran to the station with the money and a gas can. He returned after two hours when it should have taken fifteen minutes, and we fulfilled our side of the contract, thanking them profusely for trusting us.

"Gas stations are running empty. I had to go to the next closest and wait in line," Dad explained.

"I guess we're out of business."

"Guess so," Dad said. "But it wasn't anything we did or for a lack of trying."

He put his arm over my shoulders as we walked home in silence even though I was almost as tall as him. He had me by a good fifty pounds, although he was much thinner now than when the summer started.

A week after the mysterious craft entered orbit and a capsule delivered by a Falcon 9 tried to rendezvous and failed, the neighborhood was eerily quiet. Everyone had retreated into their homes. For that week, the world stopped.

Mom and Dad went house to house to make sure our neighbors were okay. We had learned to stretch what we had so we still had plenty of food.

On the eighth day, the neighbors started stopping by for lunch, the biggest meal of the day. We set up our kitchen like a buffet and delivered lean soup with meat and homemade muffins. Many ate like they were starved.

I think they might have been.

On the tenth day, the mysterious craft left orbit and accelerated away, taking the same path out of the solar system that it had followed in.

On the twelfth day, the government implored everyone to go back to work. The crisis was over. A new commission had been formed to study the phenomena.

After two weeks, Mom and Dad closed the lunch buffet. We had work to do. People went to their jobs as if nothing had changed.

"How did that affect anyone? No one died. No laser beams from space. Nothing." I tried to wrap my head around it.

And failed.

"Crisis is a window into the soul," Dad explained. "And most crises are manufactured to take our eye off what is really happening. Like this alien craft. It was something important and the puppet masters had nothing else they could point at to distract us. Maybe the emperor has no clothes after all."

I understood, finally. How does it affect us? Because they told us it did, when it didn't. Sleight of hand. I found I was just like my parents. I liked what I could see and preferred actions over words.

I clapped my dad on the shoulder. "Then that emperor can't work for me because who wants a naked person cutting their lawn?"

Dad laughed. "You're almost there. It would be a naked guy telling them he's cutting the lawn, when he's not. In reality, he bought a goat that may eventually come through and trim things."

Like I had learned from Mrs. Johnson, the older people got, the smarter they got. It would take me a while to unpack what Dad had said, but I had lots of time. There was still a week of grass cutting left before school.

ABOUT THE AUTHOR

International Bestselling Science Fiction Author

https://craigmartelle.com

https://www.facebook.com/AuthorCraigMartelle/

Craig Martelle

I'm retired from the Marine Corps, retired from my retirement gig as a lawyer, and now I work full-time as an author. I have a number of bestselling novels in categories that matter to me - Space Opera, Military Sci-Fi, Space Marine, and Post-Apocalyptic. As a serial daydreamer, it's nice to finally get the stories on paper (virtual and digital, that is).

My short story "Day of Reckoning" received first place in the Skagit Valley Writers League 2021 Literary Awards for Short Story Fiction. I write short stories in order to sharpen my writing quality because of the laser focus needed in the short form.

Ann Bodle-Nash

EXISTING IN A TIME OF PANDEMIC

March 2020

It's raining. The darkness of the day accentuates the uncertainty of the times as I sit at my kitchen table. A steady drip keeps time with my heartbeats. We are in Pandemic Time, a seemingly vast, uncharted, unlimited pause.

In front of me are the remains of two Zoom birthday party celebrations this week: hats, made of folded newspapers with stapled-on curly ribbon decorations and little snippets of tape, necessary because it has been decades since we had to fashion party hats from newspapers. Like pirates without eye patches. Yes, we wore them to add levity to our granddaughter's ninth birthday party, excitement transmitted by electronic means this year. It will be a birthday to remember. We looked very silly in the hats. The birthday girl wore a princess tiara.

The following day was our middle daughter's thirty-seventh birthday. She arrived to Zoom dressed in an inflatable Power Ranger Halloween costume. Her hair was beautiful, her smile brilliant. She had upstaged us all, as is fitting of a birthday girl. Bless that child for lifting us all up. Her cat paraded in the background, making a cameo now and then, became bored with us all and took a nap.

Yes, it's what many of us are doing while housebound. Sleeping. Cooking. Watching TV. Napping. Eating again. Checking to see if the rain has stopped, whether the tulips have survived the deer's grazing— if it's warm enough to pull weeds, plant the garden, remove moss from the driveway.

My Oregon sister is busying sewing masks for her daughter—a doctor in Indiana—who has sent out a plea for PPEs. A phrase we did not commonly know until the Pandemic. My California sister is busy tending to our at-risk parents—who live in an adult community— at ages 93 and 92. She worries the front desk will deny her entry one of these days, although she and they remain healthy. Additionally she checks progress on her house under construction, a house rising from the ashes of the Northern California Tubbs Fire of 2017.

"Isn't it enough," she says, "that we have come through the fire, and almost another one the following year? And now a Pandemic?"

I have no answer for her except to feel sympathy, and to shout YES. We are tired and it is too much already. But we continue to breathe.

Our children are scattered by this Pandemic. Our son and his wife live across the now-closed Canadian border, working from home. Our eldest daughter and her husband work as front-line responders in health care near Seattle. They disinfect obsessively to protect themselves and their only child. Our middle daughter is unemployed, awaiting an interview that was disrupted by the closing of the U.S. border and her potential employer's return to Denmark.

Husband, who is retired following a stroke—but well enough to feel the walls closing in—bought a wire, suet-cake type birdfeeder last week and took great care in positioning it outside the dining room window where we can watch obsessively. We are not birders in any sense of the phrase, but the lure of bird identification has sucked us in. The Pederson Field Guide sits on the table at the ready. Chickadees? Speckled Towhees? Downy Woodpecker? Flicker? I check online. I examine each posted photo on the birders Facebook page. It passes the time.

Friends share photos of food we have turned to in this time of Pandemic. This time of too much time, what to do, what to make? Cakes, pies, poached-pear cobbler, cinnamon bread, braided challah loaves. We crack open jars of home-canned pears, jam and pickles, grateful for our stash.

Some days we stand outside, near our rural mailbox, waiting for a neighbor to pass by, walking their dog. It happens now and then. I have met Leo, Mona and their owners, and am particularly taken with Leo. He wriggles with joy when I call out to him. I have never been a dog person, but now I feel a shift taking place. I've been carrying dog biscuits, realizing it helps bridge the friendship gap between dogs and humans.

I have met the new next-door neighbor Eric, who is sheltering in place with his 92-year-old father. And the man who lost his wife, sold his boat, bought a small house near the park, with his rescue dog from Mexico. He helped us put back together the flag on our mailbox, which had rusted, needed repainting, and now reinstallation. It is a fish motif. We kept our distance. Small mercies.

The mailman should be surprised to see it finally back up. It took a Pandemic to get around to that job.

I'm working from home, hosting radio interviews about suddenly important subjects, for our station that is locked down, on a closed college campus. Electronic wizards keep us functioning in a Zoom sort of way. I play music to myself—with no way to broadcast—but have decided John Denver is too nostalgic (it makes me long for my younger days, and cry), Aretha is uplifting, Joan Baez somewhere in between. I'm on a John Prine binge to send psychic empathy towards Nashville where he struggles with Covid-19. Hello Out There, John. Sadly he did not survive.

Not everyone is housebound. The first responders are working to save us all. The least we can do is cooperate. We are all in this together.

II

May 2020

The cinnamon bread dough is rising again. It's raining lightly. I should be making vertical marks on the recipe card to represent the number of loaves I have made, two per week, since the stay-at-home-order due to Covid-19 began. I imagine I am marking on a prison-cell wall—not marking off the days, weeks or months of confinement, but the number of times I have turned on my red Kitchen-Aid mixer, combined flour, yeast, sugar, eggs and liquid, prepared the cinnamon-sugar filling, and placed the greased bowl in the warmth of the closed-door microwave oven to rise.

There is not much else to do some days. We are retired. We are deemed at increased risk of infection to an unseen enemy. It feels to be a powerful force, the likes of which we have never before faced.

Covid-19 is not understood as well as Malaria or the long list of sexually transmitted diseases. Polio is a distant memory. TB rarely mentioned. Small pox prevention a small scar on my left shoulder. At best Covid's mark may be internal, a psychic scarring; at worst death or long-lingering symptoms.

I have resumed my weekly radio station DJ duties as Ann the Bohemian, remotely spinning electronic mp3s. In the Before Times I carried a heavy bag of CDs to the station each Tuesday afternoon, decided which cuts to play, and spontaneously composed a program. Now I tell my unseen listeners, "I'm coming from my kitchen to yours." Truth. Now I spend hours gathering the cuts, recording, uploading to a server, and trying to sound upbeat, never sure who is listening. Sometimes I get fan emails from my neighbors. My cover is blown.

Yet, my garden is flourishing. Peas are sending tendrils skyward, beans emerging—rhubarb spreading its massive leaves wide, covering parsley and thyme. Or perhaps it's oregano, I've lost track. So much is mushing together in my memory as the days run into one another. We now have five bird feeders, each with specific food based on the configuration of the feeder. I'm meeting new species daily, taking photos through the window and posting them to my neighbor Becky for confirmation. My bird guru.

Driving the fourteen miles to town, I realize going to the grocery store has become a major, weekly, entertaining event. Costco? Hell yes. Trader Joes, double yes. We wear our required masks and stand in line to enter—shop quietly, rarely making eye contact—follow one-way arrows, delight in the tomatoes, bananas, the frozen pot stickers. We feel lucky to have the funds to buy more food than the basics—to have remained healthy.

Is this week eight we ask each other? Will the stay-at-home order ever lift? It has become the norm, but what would it be like to dine in a restaurant again?

My Oregon sister calls and asks if I'd like to travel with her to Iceland at the end of the summer. She might as well be asking if I'd like a trip to the moon. I, the non-stop traveller as long as I have been alive (nearly), decline. "I'm waiting on the vaccine," I say. It may be a long time. It may be forever. I stumble upon travel photos in my hard drive and I feel the tug, now tempered with fear instead of excitement to take on the world. Paris toujours, has become a perhaps.

The tulips are finished, roses budded but not in bloom, the rhododendrons mid-way through their annual spectacle: first white, then pink, red, purple. I do not understand why the color progression is that way—I only observe nature's order year after year. I take comfort in the reemergence of hostas, ferns breaking from dark, damp earth and bleeding hearts, astilbe, fuchsias, calendulas, hollyhocks, gladiolas, volunteer tomatoes and dill. Potatoes popping up where I did not expect.

There is an order to nature, of that I feel certain. But this year we are caught in a maelstrom of nature gone berserk—tossing us about, while we hang on tight, seeking the shore, which is not yet visible. I dream of that order, wishing it to return, and to please hurry. I am dreaming of Greece, or France, or Yellowstone, or a long car ride most anywhere.

III

September 2020

Fall has arrived in the Northwest. But Pandemic Fall is different than others in my memory. We have those expected warm days, and a smattering of raindrops. But this year it's the smoke that has us hunkered down, like rabbits in their burrows. Smoke that engulfs us from fires throughout the West: California, Oregon, Washington. The air so thick I've lost sight of my next-door neighbor's home, on the other side of a long blackberry hedge, and a volunteer apple tree brimming with mystery apples. The wind will surely shift eventually, and blow from the Pacific toward the Cascades, toward the Rockies and the Appalachians. But it takes its time this year.

Ironically it's a bumper year for my fruit trees— apples and pears galore. Any neighbor who inquires receives a bag of multiple varieties. Organic I remind them. Translation: they may be buggy.

We now don our masks because of smoke when we take out the garbage, quite accustomed to mask wearing— in fact I have a bag full of choices. I made three styles as the Internet downloads progressed.

Limited Edition 1: rectangles with long ties behind the head with pleats. Signed and numbered.

Limited Edition 2: rectangles with a pieced rounded beak, loops of elastic at the ears (never quite the correct length), and a twisty tie (like in the produce department, only white) inserted into a top seam.

Limited Edition 3: Finesse now at play—beak style, elastic loops extra long and self-adjustable by way of a loose knot, with bendable nose metal. Reversible, sometimes with two different fabrics joined together across the front. Children's length and adult sized. Oversized for two friends with beards. Batiks are my game: fish prints, paisleys, eggplants, pineapples, polka dots, fish rings, and sloths. Brown geometrics for a neighbor. All with three layers, including one layer of iron-on, fused (not woven), interfacing. CDC guidelines.

I have put my sewing machine away for now. The energy for creation has subsided as the pandemic season stretches before me. Besides, commercial mask makers have flooded the Internet, grocery, Target, gas stations, even the feed store. Mass production has overtaken my desire to create custom designs and fabrics. I still give a nod to those sporting homemade masks when I pass them in the grocery—out of respect.

But the loneliness of isolation persists. There are friendship bubbles for some, school pods, and organizational meetings via Zoom. There is my son on the other side of a closed Canadian-US Border. A scant fifty miles north, it might as well be 5,000 miles for all the progress that has not been made since March, when it slammed shut. I definitely heard the thud and the key turn in the lock. Heard the key falling down a dark, deep well. Now I hear there are 400,000 Canadian RVs headed for British Columbia, to winter, instead of Arizona. It's warmer than Alberta.

The granddaughter is back in school, but remotely. Grade 4 will be remembered, not for who was in her class, but for which adult monitored her learning each day. The upside is those now-possible bike rides during the lunch break.

Middle daughter has a new job in her field, after months on unemployment. She has a boyfriend, found in these times! He is kind and knows how to fix things. Bonus points.

We are allowed to see our granddaughter and eldest daughter again, and to steal a forbidden hug, if her father is not watching. It is touch we are missing—we vulnerable older adults. Our children—for our safety—are debating upcoming holidays.

But there has been death among us. The cornerstone of my September 2020, Pandemic-Time memory is my father's passing. Covid-19 or not, the natural life and death cycle keeps playing out. Even though 94, even though he was struggling for many months (years), even though he was lucky enough to have my mother, and daughters and faithful caregivers tending to him, the loss is deeper than I expected. When a friend says, "I'm so sorry for your loss," I unexpectedly tear up. It catches me off guard every time. My friends notice, and sigh, and say, "It just takes time. "They have already walked the path of parental loss.

In this time of Pandemic—with over two hundred eighty thousand US deaths at this writing—political election conflicts, parental loss, fires that rage again in my hometown and isolation from old friends and family—nature has never called more strongly as an antidote. The soothing sound of moving water, goldfinches and great blue herons singing out, an eagle soaring above, a mysterious overfed-Siamese cat appearing at my doorstep all mean something. Just what, I am not yet sure. Perhaps that if we settle in for the long haul we too will survive.

IV

March 2021

Vaccination

We watched, listened and waited for the Vaccine. For our turn to be called to the medical altar—to be saved. First they named eligible the seventy-five and over in Washington State. We watched the chaos nationally unfold, every state with varying eligibility standards.

Facebook became a modern-day telegraph, with friends posting photos from Florida as they had the *Jab*, as it began to be called. With fits of envy and jealously those not from Florida questioned why Floridians were able to line up in the heat for their shots, while we in colder and more Blue States were still on stay-at-home orders, with restaurants, gyms, bowling alleys, churches, movie theatres and most other forms of entertainment closed, except for take-out restaurant meals. We were now accustomed to ordering Thai food, picking it up at the window and eating it with plastic utensils in our car, while still hot. We were tired of home cooking, tired of staring blankly across the dinner table at one another, again. We craved being out in the world.

It was not the mask wearing that upset me. No, we were accustomed to the masks, and had various styles ever present in the car, elastic draped over the gearshift knob. It was the forgetting. Sometimes I would start into the grocery store—keys already placed in my purse or pocket, halfway to the entrance door—and pass another shopper masked snugly. I would do a turnaround, reopen my car and grab a mask, chiding myself for not remembering automatically after a year of masking up.

How many repetitions does it take to establish a new routine? Scientific estimates vary. Consider this:

you rearrange a drawer in the kitchen, moving the contents, and two months later you are automatically, unthinkingly, still searching the former location for that utensil. Or something in the bathroom cupboard. Or in your garage. Humans are slow to adapt, although we try.

Phillippa Lally, health psychology researcher at University College London, published a study in the European Journal of Social Psychology noting, "On average, it takes more than 2 months before a new behavior becomes automatic — sixty-six days to be exact. And how long it takes a new habit to form can vary widely depending on the behavior, the person, and the circumstances." In Lally's study, it took anywhere from eighteen days to two hundred twenty-four days for people to form a new habit.

In light of this study I try to be patient with myself, to develop a compensatory strategy, like leaving a mask in the pocket of jackets I am likely to wear to town, or stuff one in my purse or backpack. I hope to reach that magic sixty-six -attempts-to-remember-the-mask mark soon.

In mid-January a palpable shift begins. Sixty-five and older becomes the new baseline for vaccination eligibility in our state. On day one of our possibilities I attempt to book appointments for my husband and me. The following day we drive thirty miles to a medical clinic in a nearby town. Giddy with subdued excitement (and a little apprehension) we approach, take the elevator to the second floor, and enter a festive world of happiness, akin to a cruise ship departure lounge. The demographic unfolds: elderly, neatly dressed with a sense of anticipation— husbands, wives, friends, strangers gathered together. Ready for the cruise to freedom. The freedom to hug our children, grandchildren, and friends again. To touch.

The attendant takes us together to a cubicle. We sign waivers. We designate which arm is to receive the miracle drug, hoping it will do as promoted, as promised. We believe in the science of the CDC and our hero Dr. Fauci.

The nurse gives us a sticker and our immunization certificate and we smile, and feel an unseen burden lift. We float to the waiting room, sit six feet apart from the others for fifteen minutes— everyone chatty, relieved, smiling. Ready now for that cruise to the future, without Covid constraints. Of course we still wear masks in public, wash our hands, wipe down the grocery cart handles with disinfectant, stand on the six-foot distance markers at the checkout line, remain on our side of the acrylic shields (speaking loudly through the slight opening to be heard). We discuss our failing hearing.

After a month the second dose is injected, and we breathe. We wait the additional two weeks for full effect. And then suddenly soft talk of travel begins to be heard.

Our neighbor Nora is moving across country and a farewell party is held in another neighbor's backyard, in fifty-three-degree weather, under a canopy because it has been raining. We quiz her about the logistics. She has a plan for her nine-day journey with her son and her Great White Pyrenees dog, in a rental van. I am jealous. My adventurous spirit is rising.

I say, "Some are travelling to Mexico I hear!" Heads nod.

Nurith says, "I'm flying to the East Coast Wednesday to see my daughter and her family. I just want to hug them." We nod.

Another says, "I bought a ticket to Connecticut for August! I might have to cancel, who knows?"

I say, "I hear it's warm in Palm Springs now." The sun has popped out as we sit beside an outdoor fire pit, blocking ash and smoke from our eyes. I'm wearing a sweatshirt and a down jacket and wool socks but imagining capris, sandals. I've never been to Palm Springs. I don't mention I already have a ticket.

Unfortunately, our traveling companion falls down her spiral staircase and breaks her back, five days prior to our scheduled departure. The trip vanishes, like a transitory dream, despite her demands we continue on without her as she languishes in the hospital. I do not want to go without her so I plant potatoes and onions in my garden instead.

It feels foreign to be making plans to go anywhere outside our county. But I feel the power of vaccination surging, allowing me to dream of entry into the world, although not really *The World.* Italy is back on lockdown, France has yet to have a successful rollout of vaccines, and Germany is trying. Canada is vaccinating those over eighty. There are upticks in fifteen U.S. States that have relaxed mask requirements, hosted spring breaks, reopened restaurants, bars, and clubs. Our son in Canada is still in lockdown—mid-summer the target date for thirty-something's, he says. I feel ashamed. Remarkably he receives the vaccine ahead of predictions.

There is no Before Time now, just post-vaccination time for those lucky enough to have age on their side. And yet the threat is not subdued entirely; it lurks.

Nature calms me. My garden is planted with the early crops—carrots, lettuce, beets, snow peas.

Rhubarb crowns are emerging, daffodils cheerful, tulips hopeful. I again shoo deer and bunnies from my yard, string plastic fence around deer-favorite flowers, do the quiet chores that have become our life. On rainy days and nights we binge on Netflix, discovering new series, like Call My Agent and Atypical. It's easy to be lost in the world of French movie agents and a family on the spectrum. We watch The Bachelor, with the Matt and Rachael debacle, and The Prince Harry and Meghan interview with Oprah, reflecting on race in America. We consider justice in America and encourage conversations in our family, knowing it touches us all including my sister's family with an adopted Chinese daughter and her son's biracial girlfriend.

It's difficult to emerge from our cocoons after a year of hibernation and altered realities. We are forever changed, scarred, and marked. We are all survivors, mourning the loss of friends and family and unknown others.

My watercolor sketches continue to show improvement, although perspective generally eludes me. But I keep sending postcard-sized paintings to my mother who I hope is saving them, for it may be my most visible documentation of this time. The time we took a collective deep breath and held it for a year. The time I began to consider the power of prayer to protect and to sustain us—masked of course.

ABOUT THE AUTHOR

Ann Bodle-Nash is a writer of both fiction and narrative non-fiction, who lives with her husband on Samish Island along the Salish Sea, with a view of evergreens, blackberry vines and wildlife. She often writes travel posts from around the world, with an eye towards the unusual.

She holds an MFA in Creative Writing from the Rainier Writing Workshop at PLU in Tacoma, Washington (2018).

Her story "Existing in a Time of Pandemic" received first place in the Skagit Valley Writers League 2021 Literary Awards for Creative Nonfiction.

Much of her other published work can be seen in the literary journals Sharkreef.org, Indieitpress.com

Ann can be reached via email   annnash51@gmail.com

Deborah McClendon Magnuson

BOOTSTRAPS

Pull yourself up by your own bootstraps, they said.
Easy to say when you're warm, housed, and fed.
My boots have no straps, so what can I do?
My boots are just the wrong kind of shoe:
Some straps are too small, and break when I try
Frayed to a remnant the incorrect size;
Sometimes they're uneven; can't get a good grip;
If the straps are too long, come undone, then you trip.
A veteran's boots, filled with dried blood,
Bring flashbacks of nights on patrol in the mud.
Some boots the wrong color, others too small.
What about those who have no boots at all?

Deborah McClendon Magnuson

SINGING FOR THE JOY OF IT

Returning to college after time away is not the snap they promised in the brochure, Jill muttered. She strode across the quadrangle, dodging drizzle, to the Fine Arts Building, hoping she would be on time for her audition. Depending on the results, she would be in either the touring Chamber Choir, the Concert Choir, or the Hutton College Singers. With Ed 300 (Experience-Based Teacher Training) at eight am three days a week, Ed 426 (Elementary Reading Instruction) two days a week, a practicum and seminar to be scheduled, Psych 425 (Tests and Measurements) two days a week, and work in the Ed Office in between, her schedule was open for any one of the three.

Whatever happens. After hearing the Chamber Choir in concert last year, she didn't know if she would make it. Jill had done nothing but church choirs since she and her sister Pat went to the University together. *It all depends on what Professor Wolff decides. It's not like I want to try to be a music major again.* She had been too shy at the concert to go up afterward and introduce herself to the director, although her friend Kate had. She wanted to tell him just how much she had enjoyed the music, and how it had influenced her coming to Hutton College. She knew there were other choirs at other places, and she had been more influenced by the education program, but the concert had been a factor. At least the music reminded her how much she wanted to go back to school.

More mock-Corinthian columns framed the entrance to the Fine Arts Building as she walked through the double doors to the atrium with its vaulted ceiling. Signs invited her to browse the student exhibits in the Hutton College Gallery to her left, but she wanted the directory, so she could go to the choral room for her audition with time to spare. The gallery could wait until later. According to the directory, the choral practice room was on the third floor, Room 398. Jill walked to the staircase spiraling at the end of the hall, her footsteps echoing on the parquet floor. The first floor seemed to be a more public place with the gallery, the theatre, and no classrooms anywhere in sight. It was still before eight in the morning, the time for her audition, but that part was nearly empty. *Maybe that's better. No matter how this audition goes, I'll have only myself to blame.*

The stairway and the corridor seemed unusually long, but she finally found the room marked "398: Choral Practice." She was still early enough to glance at a miniature oil painting hung on the opposite wall from the door. It depicted a musical scene from the times when people still gathered in groups to sing for recreation. A quartet assembled in a music room during the Victorian era, judging from the clothing style. Both the gentleman directing from the piano and the gentleman standing by the piano, dressed in a cream-colored cutaway suit, were dandies. The blonde beauty singing from the portrait chair held a large spray of deep magenta roses, and her auburn-haired companion, seated on the opposite couch, held an unplayed lute in her sapphire-gowned lap. *You look like you are all singing for the joy of it,* she mused as she cracked open the door to the choral room.

"Well, come all the way in if you are going to, "said a man gruffly. Jill shielded her eyes against the early-morning sunlight through the large bay window. She could see him now, in outline, seated at the baby grand piano.

"I'm here for a choral audition." She had interrupted the pianist at his work.

"So you are, and a little early, too." He smiled at her as she came further into the room. "I am Nathaniel Wolff." She had not seen him outside the concert, dressed that evening in tie and tails, and she had only seen him from a distance, a somewhat anonymous figure with a baton coaxing glorious music from fifty singers. Closer today, he was a short, powerfully built man, apparently in his mid-sixties, with iron-gray hair curling below the collar of his open-necked beige shirt. He nodded at Jill from the piano. "Are you ready to begin?"

"Yes, "she murmured cautiously. "I'm Jill Edwards." He made a checkmark on a paper-clipped sheet of paper on top of the closed piano and inclined his head slightly. "We will begin with scales. What part do you sing, Miss Edwards?"

"I'm an alto, I think."

He played a simple five-note scale, ascending and descending. "Keep going up the scale as it is comfortable for you. I will stop you when I hear strain in your voice, so try and be as relaxed as possible."

He played, and she sang, going up higher and higher. "You're an alto, you say?"

"I've always sung the alto part because they've needed someone to sing parts, "she explained.

"Hmm, "he said, looking at her. "Now I want you to sing a simple song, a children's song perhaps. Do you have any favorites?"

Jill smiled, relieved that he didn't ask her to sing anything technical. "I know many children's songs. What about 'Twinkle, Twinkle, Little Star'?"

"Fine. Just sing, and I'll pick up your key on the piano."

Jill began singing, and by the time she was on the second line, she heard a piano part, then the instructor singing with her in a raspy bass, not unlike his speaking voice. "I don't think you're an alto, Miss Edwards, maybe a mezzo, but we'll see." He paused and stood up in dismissal.

"I have many more to audition today and will be posting the members of all three choral groups outside this room at three today after the auditions are complete. Thank you for your time, and I will see you in class tomorrow."

Jill left at 8:20, with plenty of time before she had to report for work. She glanced again at the tableau of singers relaxing. *I'll be back*, she vowed. *I don't know where, but I'll be back.*

After her shift ended in the Ed Office, she ran across the quadrangle to the Fine Arts Building and up the stairs. *How silly,* she chided herself. *What if he hasn't posted the results yet?*

Academic time or not, Professor Wolff was as good as his word. So, although nothing was on the bulletin board outside the choral room when Jill came for her audition, she saw her name listed under Soprano II in the Chamber Choir, in the last position, but at least it was there. Jill felt she had earned a cup of hot chocolate in the coffee shop on the second floor. She sat at a table for one in a small, raised nook, where she had a good view of the entire room, but no one could see her. Of course, her mother and Pat would be upset at her people-watching if they were here.

At least she hoped no one would see her. From five tables away, she heard the familiar voice of Professor Wolff rasp, "What brings you here to this neck of the woods?" He sat, holding his coffee cup, at the table opposite a silver-haired woman picking at a salad. The table was half in shadow, so Jill wasn't sure who the woman was until she heard her voice. Jill felt her face curl in a grimace. *My major advisor and the choir director sitting at the same table.*

"I came to look at the student exhibits in the Gallery. Some of them are very interesting and not derivative at all, as student exhibits often are. Then I decided to stop for a late lunch, away from my desk." Dr. Helme-Kingston smiled at Professor Wolff and took another bite of salad.

"I need a break too, "he remarked, absently stirring his coffee. "How is your semester shaping up,

49

Kari?" He took an experimental sip, nodded, and savored it.

"I've only met with two of my classes so far, but this semester proves to be an interesting one. What about you, any musical plans yet?"

"I just finished choral auditions and posted the results, which means that soon I'll hear them sing together. Then, of course, what we do will depend on how the students sound, but I think at this point, they and the audience will expect something traditional."

She took a sip out of her steaming cup. "You must admit, Nate, that audiences do like harmonies that make sense."

He wagged a pointed finger back at his companion. "You would say nothing else, even though I know you are capable of something a little more avant-garde." He sipped his coffee again. "I ran into Mei-Pa Chao at a choral conference a few weeks ago, and that reminded me. He had his touring choir sing selections from the Beethoven Mass in C a few years ago. They did Brahms' German Requiem about the same time. You know it, don't you, Kari?"

Jill paused, frozen, as her advisor glanced around the room to see if anyone was watching. Seeing no one, she sang the melody line to "How lovely is Thy dwelling place" in a strong contralto, sotto voce.

"Well, that answers my question," he commented, smiling. "You shouldn't worry so much. In this building, no one would give it a second thought, and you certainly have a better voice even now than I ever did."

Jill knew that she would not move from her spot until they left. As a former music major, she could hear technique and intonation. Jill doubted that Dr. Helme-Kingston would be self-conscious, but she knew she was. It was just another facet of her instructor's personality, and it did explain her speaking voice.

The next day, Jill walked across the quadrangle to the Fine Arts Building for the first meeting of the chamber choir. Despite herself, she was excited. *I can't imagine how I made it in,* she wondered as she passed the vocal quartet on the wall, *but I told you I'd be back, and here I am.*

When she opened the door to the choral practice room, almost 50 students were milling around the room. A tall, thin man about her age, with longish brown hair and sideburns, rapped the side of a music stand, and the clang got everyone's attention. Most of the buzz stopped. He spoke in a high tenor voice, "My name is Dale Mervin, and I am Professor Wolff's assistant. Before he comes in, please find your respective sections. Sopranos are upfront on my right, with tenors in the rows behind them. Altos are to my left with basses behind them. Once you are all in your sections, I will distribute your folders and start a seating arrangement."

A tall blonde in green drawled, "My, my, Dale, so officious already. Don't mind him, kids, you know what they say about a little power."

She grinned when Dale glared at her. "Y'all heard the boy now. Let's find our sections like adults. Altos, you're with me." She commented to the redhead next to her, "Just like a line of ducklings following their mama."

51

Dale raised his voice again. "I will come around to each section with folders to seat you in your positions based on your audition."

Some people knew one another, but Jill went over by the soprano section and stood by the wall, knowing no one, and that she was one of the last to be chosen. Just then, Dale came by with a stack of folders. "When I call your name, please come and take your folder and find a chair." There were 12 in the soprano section, and Jill patiently waited her turn. At last, he handed folders to Julia Edwards and a short brunette named Caroline Wise. Caroline and Jill found seats next to each other in the back of the section and grinned, like those thrown together often do. "Well, at least we've made it. Cynthia Wise, the first name Dale called, is my cousin and probably one of the soloists this year. I doubt that I'll ever be one, even when it's time for my senior recital."

She laughed when Jill looked puzzled. "Why am I studying music too when I'll always be in Cindy's shadow? I play the piano much better than she does. "

Professor Wolff opened the door. As he strutted across the room, students stood for the director. Then, he inclined his head and motioned to them to sit down.

"I see that Dale has already organized you. In that case, I will introduce him and some advanced students in choir this year." He gestured to Dale. "Dale Mervin is a countertenor and my assistant this year. Advanced sopranos include Cynthia Wise and Nasreen Farhana." "Many of you already know Cindy but Miss Farhana is new to us. She just transferred to Hutton College from the San Francisco Conservatory of Music to finish her education." *Must be a story there,* Jill wondered. *There are plenty of places in the area where someone could go to school, I guess.*

"Advanced contraltos include Linda Fenton and Sue Bohannon."

Linda waved, and Jill recognized the tall blonde and her redhaired neighbor. "You've already met Dale, and you will undoubtedly come to know the advanced students better in the coming months, as some of them are also your section leaders. Now, the purpose of a choral group is to sing. I begin each session with vocalise as a transition to relax and to stretch your voices." He nodded to Dale at the piano, who began playing five-note scales in the typical up and down pattern. "In this first group, all of you will sing in unison. Then, altos and basses, feel free to drop out when it becomes too high for you."

Jill reflected, "*It will get too high for me soon enough,*" as she sang with the rest of the sopranos. Despite what Caroline had told her, she had a lovely voice and kept singing upward until the advanced students in the soprano section, two other sopranos, and a few tenors were left.

"Now, I will change the pattern to another one, once again to sing in unison. Dale will demonstrate it for you."

Dale stood relaxed while everyone else listened intently. Although Jill did not like his attitude, she had to admit he had a beautiful voice, unusually high and sweet for a male whose voice had changed. He tossed his head to one side, brushing back a long strand of hair. Jill saw Caroline grimace, then change her facial expression to an attentive smile. As Dale sang the pattern, a few of the returning students smiled in recognition. Jill herself vaguely recognized it and sang along with the others until it again went too high, and she had to drop out.

After the highest voices finished, Professor Wolff remarked, "I've noticed that some of you in the soprano and tenor sections dropped out when the music became too high for you. That is not a problem at this point. It is much better to sing the notes you can sing with a relaxed voice than to strain for them. You will find with regular exercise that you will be able to sing them easily later in the semester."

Dale, still seated at the piano, played a complicated series of arpeggios. The director turned toward the piano and nodded his head once to Dale, who went to join the tenor section.

"Now, you are going to do a different type of activity, one that demands all of you to listen closely to one another, blend as one voice while singing in chords and move as one voice when those chords change. This will be the last part of your vocalise before working on rehearsal music."

He played one low note on the piano, and the basses sang it, then another in harmony for the tenors, the altos, and finally the sopranos.

"I will add some divisi in later class meetings," he declared. As the piano chord faded away, he stood and began directing the choir as they, holding the same chord, swelled to forte, diminished, and then increased to middle voice. He then played another series of notes on the piano so that the chord moved to a minor key, directed them to move more slowly, and stood listening as they held the notes. Finally, he motioned them to stop. "Some of you are trying to outsing each other, and I can certainly hear it. Stop vying for my attention. All of you passed the auditions, or else you would not be here. Now try it again."

Once more, he played the bass note, this time waiting for the basses to all sing together before adding the tenor harmony note, and then waited for the tenors to sing together. Next, he added the altos slowly, and at last, the sopranos. For long moments, the choir sustained the chord, and then he played a note for the tenors to move, then the altos, then the sopranos. They all held that chord, and he directed them to swell that chord again and diminish slowly and gradually until, at last, the notes died away. Then, he repeated the procedure for several more chords.

At last, he smiled and motioned to the choir to sit. "Not bad for vocalise the first day. You still have a long way to go before you can sing as one voice in harmony, but you will get there. Right now all of you have empty music folders. Believe me; they will be full before long. Each section leader has music they will be distributing. As each piece reaches you, please put a copy in your folder."

Cynthia Wise was the section leader for the soprano section. She began passing out music folios, including a paperbound pamphlet with a red cover: Chichester Psalms by Leonard Bernstein. Jill hadn't realized that Bernstein had composed choral music other than his musicals.

Professor Wolff remarked when everyone had gotten their music folders in their sections. "I am certain that all of you have heard of Leonard Bernstein." Most students nodded vigorously. "He composed this work," holding up the red folio, "in 1965 as a choral work for the music festival that bears its name. We will probably perform it with members of the orchestra as the centerpiece of our holiday concert, so I want you to begin familiarizing yourselves with it now. Some of the tempi are a little unusual, and the words are in Hebrew."

He paused to emphasize what that might mean to rehearsals. "Not to worry for those of you unfamiliar with the Hebrew alphabet. Maestro Bernstein has transliterated the words and given us a pronunciation guide at the beginning of the work. In addition, some of you may have noticed that he intended the work originally for an all-male choir, with young boys singing the soprano and alto parts. We will not do that here, nor was that done in the world premiere performance in Philharmonic Hall. Instead, the women will sing the soprano and alto parts." He smiled. "We will begin reading the score through at the end of Movement 3, which is on your page 42, at the Measure 60 marking. The translation of Psalm 133: 1 is 'Behold how good and pleasant it is for brethren, and sisters too, I might add; to dwell together in unity.' Not a bad sentiment for a choral group, wouldn't you say?" He looked to see that all of us had the right books and pages, and then he asked, "Cindy Wise, please read the Hebrew words to us."

Cindy nodded and read the transliterated words, "Hineh ma tov, umah nayim, shevet achim, gam yachad," with the ch pronounced at the back of her throat. Jill, who had not taken any foreign languages since high school French, was impressed.

After a long pause, the director nodded and played the first seven-note chord, and the choir sang through the next page to the end.

Professor Wolff said, "As it took some time for you to get organized this first rehearsal, I will ask your section leaders to show you where your music folders go in the cabinets so you can put them away. You are welcome to take them with you if you wish to take a closer look at any of the music, but make sure you bring your folders with you to the next class session."

As Jill left the rehearsal room to go back to Thorndike Hall, she nodded to the painting. *I'm still not sure who you are, but I will get used to being here.*

Deborah McClendon Magnuson

RAINBOWS AND STONE

Virginia,
Your words were not enough for you,
Your words that flowed in shining streams
of incandescent sentences,
burnished and polished till each one gleams.

If you had known that after the war
reading women would choose to follow their dreams
because of you,
Would you have weighted your pockets with dull rough
stones,
walked to the river to drown?

Would you, Virginia?
Because of you,
I write and watch for the rainbow,
in opalescence diffused,
sparkling down.

In memory of Virginia Woolf (1882-1941)

ABOUT THE AUTHOR

Deborah McClendon Magnuson

Writing and music have been constants throughout my life. For the most part, my poetry has either hidden in journals, given as gifts, or handed in as assignments. Other genres include children's books in various stages, a novel-in-progress, and short articles ghostwritten online for various websites. The variety includes everything from a K-12 tutoring company to a senior living blog. My newest assignment: blurbs for a songwriting platform. My published works include my thesis from Western Washington University and co-authoring academic publications. I am such a newbie that I do not have a website of my own yet, but my email address is deborahchaya@yahoo.com. My poem "Bootstraps" is based on experiences working at the Department of Social and Health Services (DSHS) as a social worker. It received First Place in Skagit Valley Writers League 2021 Literary Awards for Poetry.

Darlene Dubay

WHAT IS IT ABOUT A ROSE?

Have you ever really seen a rose,
And known the softness of its petals?
So transient and fleeting—
And when it fades, can you feel
The sadness—resignation even—
It has acknowledging its brief glory?
You can carve in stone or paint with oils
Or fashion one of silk
But a living, breathing rose
Demands attention.
Not loudly, like a dahlia
But insistently enough to catch
An unsuspecting traveler
By throwing forth its distinctive scent
In order to entangle and entice
A busy mind.

Why do I anthropomorphize
Something as foolish as a rose?
Is there something within me
Wanting to share in its great beauty?
If that is so, I must acknowledge also,
Life is passing all too quickly—
And like a rose I want to play my part
As brief as it might be
To be the beauty captured by
The ones who pay attention.

Darlene Dubay

AN EXTRAORDINARY CRÈCHE

Alfred opened his eyes to see the sunrise coloring the ice on his windowpane, making it look like golden-pink cellophane. Around the edges of the window, frost built and crept towards the center. He jumped up, throwing the covers into a heap at the foot of the bed. Hardly noticing the cold hardwood floor, he rushed to the window.

"Wow, cool!" *The first real snow this winter! Billy and I are going to have fun jumping down from my fort.* His breath made icy patterns on the glass. Intrigued by the beautiful designs, he held his face close to the window, opened his mouth wide and breathed onto the glass. More designs appeared with each breath.

I wonder if Agnes is awake. I'm sure her windows aren't iced up. Her room downstairs is so warm. But I bet she'd love to see this.

Quickly dressing in his flannel-lined jeans and wool sweater, he hopped down the steep stairs from his attic room. Pausing at Agnes' door, he thought, *aw, she*

*wouldn't care about a little snow and ice. She'd
probably say it's boring or too cold. Or she wouldn't
want to mess up her hair. Or Mom would say she
shouldn't be out in the cold air with her asthma.*

He passed his sister's door without knocking
and ran down the steps. *I don't hear Mom and Dad.
Good. I can go out and make the first tracks. Maybe if
it's sticky snow, I can make a snowman.*

In the mudroom, his one-piece snowsuit hung
right over the heating duct. *Mom is so cool. She always
knows what I am going to need. How did she know it
was going to snow?*

Alfred grabbed a hat and mittens from the
basket, again grateful for his mother's thoughtfulness.
The cold air stabbed at his face as he opened the door.
A wonderland of white stretched out before him. The
lines and distinctions between lots and fields faded into
nothingness. The woods looked as though they were
miles away. Alfred jumped off the porch, surprised at
the lightness of the snow. The powdery white
accumulation billowed away from him with each step.
He made a row of feathery snow angels along the
walkway then, bored, he sprinted towards the woods.
He knew exactly where to find the break in the fence,
even with the snow.

He made a beeline for his tree fort. "This must
look really cool from above. I'm going to . . ." A shiny,
metallic object caught his eye just beyond his fort. *What
could that be?* Walking now, instead of running, he
approached the strange looking thing. Everything
around it had a dusting of snow, but the silver metal
cylinder was perfectly clean. Alfred walked around it,
taking large steps to measure its circumference. "About
twelve feet around," he guessed. It was just high
enough for him to rest his elbows on, about the height
of a kitchen counter. In the very center of its flat, smooth
top a miniature cow—*looks like a Jersey, just like*

62

Millers down the road have—stood, its head raised as though looking at the sky.

As he reached out to touch it, he thought he saw the cow move a little, but his hand grasped it firmly and he raised it to his face to get a closer look. It looked lifelike, every detail exactly like a real cow. It felt warm and soft to the touch—like a living creature. "This can't be. I must be imagining things." Holding it carefully as though it was alive, he ran to the house. *Just wait until I show Agnes. She loves cows.* A voice in his ear warned, "No. Don't show it to anyone yet. This is our secret."

When he entered the kitchen, his mother stood with hands on her hips frowning. She scolded, "Where have you been? You've got to get ready for church. It's the first Sunday of Advent. Hurry up, now."

"Okay, okay. I'm already dressed. I just need to eat something."

He grabbed a glass of orange juice and popped a piece of bread into the toaster. Spreading a thick layer of peanut butter on the toast once it was up, he downed the whole slice in three bites. "I'm ready."

Mom and Dad, Agnes and Alfred piled into the car for the short drive to Saint Clément's Church. The tiny cow lay forgotten in the pocket of Alfred's snowsuit. He did not remember anything about it until getting ready for bed that night. After his bath he snuck down to the mudroom to retrieve the little cow from his pocket. He reached in, feeling for it. His fingers closed around a soft, warm object and he drew it out. It was the same cow, but instead of standing with its head raised, it was lying down with its legs tucked underneath, its head drooping and eyes closed. *How could that be? I'm sure it was standing when I picked it up. Or maybe I just imagined it.*

"Good night, Mom. Good night, Dad," Alfred said as he headed up the stairs to his attic room. He was eager to examine the cow and wasn't ready to show it to anyone quite yet. He set it atop his dresser next to a Lego castle, smoothing its hair back with one finger. "Good night, Elsie."

School days that week were busy. Alfred's favorite time at school was the noon recess. The new snow gave Alfred and his sixth-grade buddies lots to do during the long lunch break. There were snowball fights, fort building and packing down an area in preparation for an ice rink. After school, before the bus picked up the students, they had time for a few trips down the sledding hill next to the school. No new snow fell all week.

On Saturday morning, just before dawn, Alfred opened his eyes sensing a change. He took his headlamp from the nightstand and aimed it at the window. Icy fingers ran along the edges of the window. "I bet there's more snow. Great!"

He turned the headlamp to light up the top of his dresser. *I wonder if Elsie is awake.* The cow was again standing, looking towards the window and the woods beyond. "This is too weird. Whoa! I have an idea. How would you like to go outside, Elsie?" It seemed to him that she nodded, or at least blinked.

He dressed and snuck down the steps and out the door, with Elsie safely in his shirt pocket. Heavy snow covered the walkway. Alfred tried to push through it, but the going was tough. "What I need is an angel to brush a path for me. I want to get to my fort to see what's happening."

As though a magic hand swept through the snow, a path of lighter, shimmery snow appeared in front of Alfred. Walking along, the snow floated up like feathers around him. Alfred only needed to follow the sparkling snow. *I don't know where it's taking me, but I feel like I'm walking on air.*

In mere seconds he was at the base of his tree fort and the same silver cylinder stood, clean and shining just beyond. In the exact center lay three, snow white sheep, so small that when he reached to pick them up, he could easily hold all three of them in both hands. "They're beautiful. Do you want to see, Elsie?" The cow moved in his pocket and Alfred took Elsie out and set her next to the sheep.

Eager once again to be in his room and examine them closely, he stuffed them into his pocket and ran home.

His mother called from the kitchen, "Breakfast is ready. I made your favorite, French toast."

"I'm not hungry, Mom. Maybe Agnes would like it."

"Well, okay, but you'll need to eat something before we go shopping. You have to buy something for your sister, and I know just the store where they have her favorite collectibles."

"I'll be ready. Just give me a minute."

Alfred ran to his room, arranged the sheep and cow in a circle on his dresser, facing each other and said as he turned to leave, "You guys be good."

Agnes stopped him at the head of the stairs. "Where have you been sneaking around this morning? I saw you go out the door, but I didn't see any tracks in the snow."

"Whatever! You just couldn't see them because I just stayed close to the house." How could he tell her about the miniature animals without sharing? He knew she collected miniature farm and village scenes. The cow would be just the thing, but . . .

Returning from the shopping trip without a gift, he promised his mother he would try again next week to find something for his sister.

"I know you don't always get along, but just think about what she might like. She can't play outside in the cold like you do."

Busy with school, there was no time to think about cows or sheep or presents for Agnes. Schoolwork focused on preparing for the holidays and finishing projects before the year's end. Again, no new snow fell during the week.

He hoped for more snow as he closed his eyes on Friday night. *Maybe there will be another surprise for me by my fort.* But in the morning, he was disappointed to see only a heavy accumulation of frost. It was beautiful hoarfrost, but Alfred wanted snow. Snow made everything magical.

The cow and sheep on his dresser were making little mooing sounds and soft baa's as though to get his attention. As he approached them, they moved to face him and nuzzled his fingers as he reached for them. "Let's go see what marvels we can find this morning, guys." They nodded in agreement.

There was no iridescent snow to lead him and no silver cylinder near his fort. The animals in his pocket, though, were moving and wriggling. He took them all out, careful not to drop them in the snow. Standing in the woods, Alfred kicked at the snow on the ground, his shoulders slumped. "No new animals are coming." He looked at the ones he was holding. "You'll have to be enough. Let's go home."

They shook their heads, "No." Then all of them looked left as though to say, "Go that way."

Alfred begrudgingly slogged through the snow in the direction the animals looked, although he had lost hope of finding anything. He held the animals in his palms until they all started jumping up and down, their motions saying, "This is it!"

Standing before an enormous stump of an ancient tree, Alfred saw nothing unusual. He walked around it. Nothing. He walked around again. Noticing indents in the tree at eye level, he thought maybe he could climb to get a look at the top. He put Elsie and the sheep in his pocket and stretched up to grab the indent. He hoisted himself up and found more indentations, almost like a ladder.

When he reached the top of the stump—almost twelve feet in the air—he peered over the edge. *Whoa! How can this be clean and dry when frost covers everything else in sight?* Alfred looked around, expecting to see another miniature animal, maybe a horse or donkey, but there was nothing. The animals in his pocket were squirming. "It's here," they all said. Alfred looked again and noticed a glowing light near the far edge of the stump. He shimmied on to the top of the stump and crawled across to the other edge, ten feet away. As he reached out to touch the light, it moved and became larger. A force lifted him from the stump and set him gently back on the ground. At the very edge of his vision, he perceived what appeared to be a person in diamond-covered clothing, but every time he turned his head, it moved just outside his peripheral vision. An inner voice said, "Don't try to see me directly, but look for what I enlighten."

"What does that mean?" Alfred asked.

"I come to announce the promised one. Wait with patience until the proper time."

Alfred wanted to ask, "Who are you talking about? Why can't I see you? Why do you talk in riddles?" But something in the gentle voice of the spirit made him hold his tongue. He stopped trying to catch sight of the—what was it? An angel! "Are you an angel?"

"Do you believe?" Alfred heard the question in his mind.

"Yes, yes of course."

Without knowing how he got there, he was standing in the mudroom, removing his clothing. "Yes, I believe," he said again.

"What do you believe?" Agnes asked. "Who are you talking to, and why did you put your clothes on and then not go outside? Is it too cold for you?"

Alfred stuck his tongue out at Agnes and wrinkled his nose. "I did . . ." Alfred almost let it slip about seeing the angel, but caught himself saying, "I didn't want to be late for my shopping trip with Mom. You want a Christmas present, don't you?" Agnes coughed. Alfred could hear her shallow, rapid breaths. In a kinder tone he said, "Maybe today I can find something for your collection that I can afford, or maybe that light blue scarf you love." *Why did she have to be so nosey?*

He ran to his room and put the animals on the dresser. The angel was nowhere in sight, but a glow of amber light pulsed around Elsie and the sheep, even after Alfred turned the light off. "Bye, guys. Be good."

Another unsuccessful shopping trip put pressure on Alfred to find something suitable for his sister's Christmas present. He already had the wood birdhouse he had made for his father wrapped and under the tree. The special chocolates he and Agnes had made for their mother were hidden in Agnes' room.

"But, Mom," he said, "How can I find something she'll really like? I don't have enough money to buy the kind of things an almost teenager would like. You know how girls are."

"Use your imagination, Alfred. You're good at imagining things."

School was out for the entire week before Christmas and Alfred's mother had lots of chores. She always assigned the dirtiest projects to Alfred. Agnes' asthma prevented her from so many things.

The house had to be scrubbed from top to bottom. The gingerbread baked for the gingerbread houses, the outdoor life-size nativity scene retrieved from storage and arranged by the front door. More decorations needed to be hung outside.

Alfred sighed, wanting to play with Billy, or at least go to his fort. "Isn't this enough already? I haven't even had time to go to my fort all week."

"That can wait until after Christmas. You'll have another week of vacation before you have to go back to school."

"But Mom..."

"No, buts. Just hand me that extension cord."

***

The animals stayed on his dresser with no more activity for the whole week before Christmas. The only thing Alfred was aware of was a glowing light over his dresser when he turned out the lights. But every morning, his mother had a list of chores for him, and he forgot about the moving animals and got right to work. She kept asking him about his plans for his sister's gift. Finally, he told her he had a something in mind. He didn't but had the impression that something would turn up.

Christmas Eve was Sunday. The children's program was presented in the afternoon after mass. Agnes sang a solo. Luckily, her asthma was under control that day. Sometimes her asthma attacks landed her in the hospital and the family kept vigil while she struggled for air. At those times, Alfred forgot how aggravating she could be. He felt sorry for her.

After reciting his memorized poem, Alfred was eager to get home. He sat through the rest of the program daydreaming about what he would get for Christmas. He planned to search through his room and wrap a recycled toy to give to Agnes. "She doesn't ever like what I give her, anyway. What's the point?"

It was dark when they finally got home, and his parents got busy in the kitchen preparing a buffet supper. His Aunt Margaret and Uncle Bill would be there shortly. Many of their neighbors usually showed up, too. Alfred went to his room to try to find just the right recycled present for Agnes. Elsie and the sheep were running around on the dresser. The angel light glittered, and music filled the room. Alfred asked, "Do you think I should check the woods one more time tonight?" Elsie and the sheep nodded vigorously, and he felt someone take him by the elbow, lead him down the stairs and through the kitchen without his parents noticing him. He quietly went out the back door.

Bright stars illuminated a glistening, snowy path, leading him a little beyond his fort. The huge cedar tree he often darted under when it was raining, glowed in a radiant light. Alfred approached, listening for unusual sounds. His heart leapt when he saw the nativity scene beneath its boughs. At least it looked like a nativity scene. He knelt in the snow for a closer look. There was a stable situated in a hollow in a huge boulder. Tiny sheep, cows, donkeys, goats and even a horse were gathered around, some sleeping, some eating and some gazing at the sky. "It's perfect, except for the people," he thought.

Alfred heard footsteps behind him. He turned to see a dark-haired boy, about his age, dropping to his knees beside him. He looked familiar. "It *is* perfect," the boy said. Or did Alfred imagine that he said it? They admired the scene, watching the miniature animals lie down, one by one.

Alfred finally felt the cold of the snow pressing though his pants. He knew he had to go home but felt glued to the spot and it was so pleasant kneeling there beside the stranger. Not looking at the boy, Alfred whispered, "Do you come here often?"

"Yes."

"I've never seen you before. What is your name?"

"I'm Manny, but Mother insists on calling me Emmanuel. That's my real name."

"Maybe we can play in my fort sometime. Where do you live?"

"Yes, I'd love that." The boy paused before answering the question. "I live on the other side…of the woods," he finally said. "I have to go now. I have some gifts to prepare for my brothers and sisters. But I know we'll meet again."

Alfred was too stunned to say anything. As the boy disappeared into the forest, an unexpected thought entered Alfred's mind. He jumped to his feet and ran back to his house. "Yes! That's perfect!" Rushing to his room he knew exactly what to do. Elsie and the sheep turned to him as he opened the door. As he lifted each one and patted its fur, tears sprang to his eyes.

"I love you guys, but you need to go and take care of my sister." He carefully wrapped each one in shiny paper. "Be good, now. Watch over her."

The angel light smiled, and Alfred was sure he heard heavenly music floating through his room.

Darlene Dubay

TWIGS AND LEAVES

The tiniest twigs and leaves so high above the roots
Of the great oak, sycamore or birch
Seem to be a separate form of life
Dancing in the light above the trunk
So unconcerned with the gravity
Of providing sustenance.
Receiving in joy life giving water
From below.
Reveling in the sun and wind
Living in the rarified air
And seeing the wideness of the world.

But cruel winds sometimes lash
And rip the little ones to float into eternity
Falling to the earth to become once again
The food that nourishes.

But the falling and the drifting,
What a thrill!

The shortness of its dancing
So brief and seeming insubstantial,
Is demeaned by solid, stern hard-workers
Who count it as a nuisance,
Who do not understand its means of giving glory.

Oh to be a leaf that gives its life so freely
Living, loving, unafraid to let go
Sailing on the winds of eternity.

ABOUT THE AUTHOR

D.M.Dubay loves the outdoors and the natural beauty of the Pacific Northwest. She expresses this love in her frequent poems about the birds, flowers, and trees. Her publications include a book of poetry: *Walking is a Prayer—Glimpses of a Spiritual Journey* and a novel, *Tales of Two Sisters*. Soon to be released is a novel about a modern-day mystic: *She Talks to Trees*. An excerpt from *Tales of Two Sisters* was published in the Skagit Valley Writers League (SVWL) Anthology *Tales for a Lazy Afternoon*.

Darlene's poem, *Last Memory of Milli* won an award in the Write on the Sound writing contest. Her short story, *An Extraordinary Crèche took second place in the first SVWL writing contest.*

Mimzi Schradi

THE PURPLE-MAROON GYM SUIT

There it hangs in my locker, like a prisoner waiting for execution. It won't be long now. One more gym class and then the dirty deed will be done. It is inevitable. It is four years in the waiting. What a way to end up. Today, shirts of famous athletes wind up in athletic halls of fame. Not so with my faithful friend. No honor, no mercy is shown. No accolades, no thanks, not even a picture will capture its glory days, except in a yearbook that will become long forgotten.

My friends, Betty, and Ruth, gather around me for the final roll call—Last time to stand at attention in the purple-maroon gym suit—the scourge of the fashion world. The cotton that will not perish, no matter how much the sweat permeates it. It tries to stay up straight and pretend that it is starched, ironed and new, but alas nothing works. Its days and hours are numbered.

After roll call by our detested gym teacher, whose name has forever been erased from my memory, except for the first name of Mavis, we march outside to play baseball in the dusty field. Sweat streams out of every pore and on to the purple-maroon gym suit.

It is a scorching June day in Highland Park, New Jersey, the last day of gym class before graduation. We have fun, clown around, but still play hard. Good habits are hard to break. When the gym bell rings, we grab the dirt-encrusted plates, balls and bats and head to the locker room where Mavis stands at the door, inspecting us, making sure we head to the showers.

As seniors, we have overcome our modesty of showering together in a large group. As freshmen it was a humiliating experience. Most of us come from homes where privacy's respected and sex is not discussed. Thirty naked bodies diving for soap and water is too much to take at first. But we get over it, as not showering equals demerits. No one wants to flunk P.E. class. Ruth has her period for months at a time and often gets out of shower detail. We tell her we smell better—our only revenge for her cunning smile.

Showering together for the last time, we giggle and share some thoughts of what to do after school—no jobs tonight, no homework, and two days of freedom before graduation. The brainstorm hits. Take Betty's car down the shore—unheard of on a school night—usually the beach is off limits then. But this is a special occasion. We won't tell anyone. Our parents will think we're at work. I'll have to let my mother in on the deal though, as only she knows where the shore house key is hidden. My mother is often privy to things other parents don't know. I think somewhere along the way, she gave up on me and let me do my thing. She raised four boys before I arrived. As I wasn't the little girl she expected, being very much the tomboy following after my older brothers, she just sort of gave up and let me have my way. My brothers often complain that she lets me do things that they were never allowed to do.

Her trust pays off, however. I won a state scholarship, which pays tuition for four years. She is rather proud of me. Especially later on, when I become the first person in my family to graduate from college. Her way of letting me find things out for myself helped me be resilient to adversity. And her love was there always, to fall back upon when things got too tough to handle.

After the final class that day or any day for that matter, we decide to meet at my house. We walk home, as cars are not allowed on school grounds, not even for seniors. Not even on the last day of classes. We stop at Betty's home first, get her car, go to Ruth's. where she gets her stuff, and then my house. Here, we find a note with a key on top. "I'm at work. Have fun. Be careful." she writes, but nonetheless gives us the okay. She adds a post-script, "Be sure to take the macaroni salad I made for you this morning."

What is she, psychic? Just like her to be so thoughtful—Mama Spanky, as my friends call her. I'm Spanky and she's Mama Spanky. Don't know when my friends started calling me that, as I'm not a leader of a gang. I guess it's because we do everything together. Well, given the blessing from my mother, we are all set. I have the key to the shore house, Betty has the key to the car—her white '57 Chevy Convertible, and Ruth has the money for gas. We load the food, our clothes, and the dreaded purple-maroon gym suit and off we go on a hot sunny afternoon.

We leave our small borough, drive over the Raritan River Bridge to New Brunswick, take Route 18 to East Brunswick and follow that until we reach Highway 33. We follow the back roads past Molly Pitcher's Well, ride down Squankum Yellow Brook Road, through Allentown and finally reach the outskirts of Point Pleasant. We turn onto River Road, over Highway 88 and a quick left turn onto Oak Street.

The "Oak Street Girls" have arrived. 2410 Oak Street. Our getaway. Our hang-out. Our path to freedom. We hurry inside the screened-in porch of the small bungalow, which is surrounded by oak trees, squirrels, and sand. I check my watch: almost five p.m., no time to waste. The beloved key opens the door; we enter the familiar knotty pine living room with that comforting musty smell. We take a deep breath and together sing, "We're here!"

We toss our bags on the beds in the back bedroom, then place our grub on the small kitchen table and in the icebox. Pushing the sliding cabinet door under the sink, I bend down and turn the facet for the well water, so the pump will work.

Once the pump is primed, we take turns using the bathroom that only fits one person, comfortably, and put on our swimsuits covered by *the purple-maroon gym suit.* Grabbing towels out of the hall closet, we slip into flip-flips, make our way out the door to head to Manasquan Bay Beach.

Betty, Ruth, and I sing more than we talk. We sing as we drive the few minutes to the beach, down to the end of River Road—the road we used to walk from grammar school through high school—before Betty had a car. Now as seniors we have wheels. The car belongs to Betty, but she includes us in all her excursions, except her dates—and occasionally then too, when we double-date or sometimes triple-date—as we do all through senior year and the first two years of college. Junior year in college, Ruth met Tom and that was the end of triple dating. She wanted him all to herself—and eventually married him—the only marriage of the three of us to last. But that's another story all by itself.

As we get out of the Chevy Convertible, we rub our hands on the side of it, taking the moment in. I think about us. *"The times are changing..."* How long will this car last? Will it last the four years the purple-maroon gym suit lasted? Being white in color, it won't fade, but what will be its fate? Will Betty know she will sell it after marriage, to get a British sporting car for her playboy husband, so they could go on rallies? Life is so precious. Maybe the gym suit knows that. Mine is beginning to itch.

I toss off inner philosophical discussions and run to join my friends at the shoreline. The beach appears deserted. Mid-week—most folks stay at home cooking dinner in the late afternoon, creatures of habit. No one goes to the beach when school is in session. However, this is our last night before graduation preparations. This is our last goodbye before summer jobs and college.

Ruth takes the first plunge into the water, walking in slowly and sinking down into the cool crisp water until she is just a ripple on the surface. I drop my towel on the sand and survey the beauty around me. *God, I love this place.* I'm relieved there is no one to see me in my purple-maroon gym suit. Maybe the people in the homes next to the public beach can, but they don't count as we can't see them, so they don't exist in our consciousness.

Across is Treasure Island—an island we often swim to from the bay beach during low tide, dodge speedboats and cabin cruisers, then hike around in the sand and through the scrub pines. I must confess I did this for several years until my twenties. It was like trying to fulfill a death wish. I wanted to be around for my children, so I stopped. I look at the ropes barely hanging above the water, surrounding the swimming area—high tide. Suddenly the beach looks small—beautiful but small. Not as expansive as the ocean or as vast as the sea—but as a child coming here, it was my world. I am leaving it today, along with my purple-maroon gym suit. I take a deep breath and run without stopping into the water, dive under and submerge the purple-maroon gym suit for the last time—this time in salt water rather than the soapsuds of my mother's old front-loading washing machine sequestered in our dusty cellar.

Betty stands still at the shore, waiting and watching.

"Come in 'Betty Boop.' The water's fine," Ruth coaxes.

"It's cold."

I am a bit more on the fleshy side, hence more resilient to the cold. "Come on Betty," I urge. "Once you get in it's fine. Just jump in. It's the only way."

Betty joins the two of us in our baptism into life beyond high school. We have cemented our friendship and will continue to be friends, no matter what, for the rest of our lives. 1963.

Where did all that time go since that day in June 1963? College. Marriage. Children. Moving away to different states. Divorces. Births, Deaths. Yet today, we remain life-long friends, although separated by thousands of miles and totally different lifestyles. And we still love the beach.

A crab bites my toe—so much for camaraderie. "I'm outta here," I yell, swimming toward the shore.

I peel off my purple-maroon gym suit like I am tearing the skin off an orange. It sticks and I have trouble getting my legs through the panties. Yes, this gym suit is no ordinary gym suit. It's a dress. In the early sixties, for girls, pants, shorts—anything vaguely masculine—is not allowed in public schools. Very repressive. Yes, the suit is a little dress, which happens to be maroon when new—now faded purple. Matching panties are worn underneath for modesty purposes. The dress has buttons down the front, a fitted waist with a belt to cinch around it, and a flared short skirt. Maroon and Grey are our school colors—The "Mighty Owls" in Maroon and Grey.

The mascot and colors suit us when we sing our fight song, "Cheer, Cheer for Highland Park High…"—in the same tune as Notre Dame's famous fight song. Over 85% of our graduating class plans to go to college—including one to Princeton, one to Vassar—not bad for children of immigrants. Betty and I will attend Douglass College, the women's branch of Rutgers University, within driving distance to our homes. Ruth chose Trenton State College—now New Jersey College—because it has such a great P.E. Department. Yes, Ruth is slated to be our representative to the P.E. infrastructure. Betty went on to be a scientist, printing business guru and bookstore owner. I went on to teach Drama and English. Teacher. Enforced poverty, but what a ride.

I smile. We are all different, have such unique interests—and we are such great friends. Highland Park…Point Pleasant—lots of memories, and good people—some I will never see again. But I know I will always see Betty and Ruth.

My good buddies come out of the water shivering. The sun is beginning to go behind a cloud; the wind is kicking up. I help them pull the sticky gym suits off their bodies. Now we just have on our wet bathing suits and sit down on our towels to dry off. No matter how cold we are, we never get into the car without dripping off. We lounge in silence on the warm sand, watch the few cabin cruisers passing by and reminisce on how we climbed on a speedboat with some guys one summer when we were freshmen, not too "bright" and without a care in the world.

Ruth laughs. "Remember we jumped over the ropes with the lifeguard blowing his whistle? We thought that boat was a ticket to paradise."

Betty groans. "What a joyride that was. The guys raced out toward the ocean with us hanging on for dear life."

I nodded. "Yes, when we got to the jetty, I nearly fell off the boat. You caught me before I sank into the drink by the rocks."

Ever the modest one, Betty laughs. "I just grabbed your arm."

"Yes, Betty, but I was scared to death, and you saved me!" Seems right then, I promised God I would never do something so stupid again if He would only take me home safely.

I start giggling, "It was fun in a weird sort of way."

Ruth grins, points to the water and laughs, "Yes, we returned to the bay in one piece, none the worse. Those older guys delivered us right back, from where we boarded their boat, dropping us off by those same ropes out there, but with no goodbyes or anything."

"I think we were a disappointment to them."

Betty nods. "Yeah, we looked better from a distance although we acted like the fourteen-year-olds we were at the time."

Unfortunately, my prayer of thanksgiving is too soon forgotten. I know as life continues, I will do more stupid things—always invoking the same prayer—If I get out of this, I will never do something so dangerous again. I think I consciously set myself up for a lifetime of tragedy. In college, my friends would call me the tragic heroine, because of the dilemmas I would get into. I would think it's because I take drama classes. They would have other reasons. If I view it as a compliment, they view it as pity. Pity, I didn't catch on then and change my ways—One disaster after another.

The cold finally gets to all of us. We pick up the pile that includes the "purple-maroon gym suit" lying in a heap in the sand. I stuff it in a paper bag I brought along for the occasion. We each intend to dump "the suit" in the trashcan as we leave the beach, but then get a common thought: *"Burn it. Make it pay for all the years of suffering and taunts from Mavis Stockington."*

Ah, there's the last name—Stocky Stockington— the woman who has an affair with Buzz La Peine, the boys' gym coach, very inept vice-principal, and not too bright teacher. I can never respect Stockington because of her hypocrisy. She always lectures us on "doing the right thing," not "fooling around with boys" and "dressing appropriately," which I assume includes the purple-maroon gym suit. Plus, she is racist—veiled, but there. She's from some hoity-toity suburb near Princeton. Thinks she's high class. We know different. And then there's Marcie Harris, the first black girl to try out for the cheer squad in Highland Park. She does not make it.

During tryouts, she asks me, "Why don't you try out, Mimzi?"

"Sorry, Marcie, I can't do a cartwheel."

What a way to think. The cheerleaders in our school are athletic, but don't have to be. They pretend to respect Stockington and look good. I don't fit into either of those categories. Marcie fits perfectly except one. She looks fantastic, but she never noses up to Stockington. She can do cartwheels and any other move you want to throw at her. She knows all the cheers—but she is Black. I still feel the guilt of not speaking up—not complaining to the higher ups or anyone about Stockington. I didn't even try out for Cheer Squad, but I am seething mad—mad because I did nothing about the unfairness of it all. I just let the power structure do its thing. What a waste of youthful spirit. Perhaps I can blame it on the times—the beginning of the sixties. The rebel in me didn't know how to act. Students did nothing to rock the boat, just conformed to society's dictates, until they woke up and exploded in college.

We hop into the Chevy and together put the top up. It is getting nippy. I ride in the back seat with the sack containing the purple-maroon gym suit. I can swear it's staring at me. Ruth turns on the radio and we sing along to our favorite oldie, "In the Still of the Night." We harmonize and do back-up for one another until we pull into the sandy side yard of the bungalow.

Cold, tired, starving, we run into the house, and do "Rock, Paper, Scissors" for dibs on the shower. I get last. Wrapping my towel around my waist, I venture outdoors, hunting for firewood. Ruth wins first rights to shower. Betty prepares the food, placing everything on the maple dining room table, near the window in the living room. I bring in wood and start a fire. Ruth comes out of the bathroom and Betty rushes in to shower in our multi-colored shower made from leftover tiles. The hot water won't last long as the shower is heated from a tank on the roof. Natural hot water—a thing of the past—like those days at the shore.

Ruth gets dressed and searches outside for hot dog sticks. I make a fire in the red brick fireplace, our cooking area for the evening. In our homes in town, none of us has a fireplace. Sitting around the fire here is always a treat.

The fire's crackling so I hop in the shower—it's colder than cold. "Burr...Freezing!" I mumble as I dry myself off and get dressed in jeans, sweatshirt, and woolen socks.

Betty and Ruth sit by the fire, barefoot, warming themselves and roasting hotdogs. "Here, Mims. We cooked you a hot dog first, as you got the icy shower."

"And..." Ruth winks at me. "We are going to let you 'do the honor' after dinner, for your suffering."

84

I smile. "Well, that's some compensation."

We begin with my mother's famous macaroni salad—she has a secret ingredient in it, which I cannot detect. Perhaps it's her love, nothing more, nothing less. Then, Polish hot dogs, slightly burned but tasty, on rolls with sauerkraut and mustard. Ruth's heritage is German, so naturally we relish that topping. When I moved out west, chili became the thing, but I still prefer sauerkraut.

We don't drink alcohol—*yet*—but partake of iced tea, prepared by my mother for our special occasion. For dessert, we chomp on Ruth's brownies— homemade and yummy. To this day, brownies are one of my favorite desserts. And Ruth still bakes from scratch—no mixes for her. Betty, our health nut, brings fresh fruit—plums, peaches, and oranges. A feast.

It is getting dark and it's getting time—time of passage—time to do the deed. Time to say goodbye— to fears, repression and grief over deeds not done. The purple-maroon gym suit—sitting in the wet paper bag, awaits its fate. I grab it and with two hands place the culprit on the now-roaring fire. Lots of smoke—we cough and sputter until it subsides. After the moisture evaporates, the flames start again—first red, then orange, then blue, then maroon and purple. I can see Ol' Mavis' face shining in the burning fire and it's not a happy face. I know it's the last time I'll see it.

After our rite of passage, Ruth tunes in the old freestanding wood radio that sits in the corner, finds the "Oldies but Goodies" station and the three of us proceed to hum along. We decide to stay the night and sleep in the living room. We open the pull-out couch that's most uncomfortable, but close to the hearth. Tonight, we will stay warm by the fire. We will spend this last night here at the shore, before venturing to our homes in Highland Park to finish the last steps for graduation—but in our own hearts and minds we have already graduated. Anything else is icing on the cake.

Mimzi Schradi

OWLS CIRCLE

Bruce and I stand in the stillness high on the upper deck among the cedars, listening to the call of the owl.

We watch a large one in flight and then a younger owl as he balances on a branch—devouring his prey.

The fading sun filters through the falling darkness and the cedar branches become a lace-filled umbrella, allowing misty rain to fall upon the mossy trees.

Nature becomes our Woodland Amphitheatre and waits for us to be seated.

Soon, other owls appear in the trees and join in song, bringing forth a sound so sweet, so melodious, my ears strain to pick up every nuance.

We take our seats, fall under the spell of the music, and listen to the grand chorale and symphony orchestra.

The "who-who's" of the basses, along with the coloratura of the spinto Spotted Owls, define the evocation of the fugue.

Then, other feathered instruments take charge.

The young flutes resonate playfully, emitting delicious melodies of pure joy.

In harmony, muffled, older trumpets echo back their triumphal theme.

The mother owls—a quartet of altos and sopranos—ease in gently, then forcefully for attention.

They coo and sing a wake-up call to their young, "Come, there is much to be done on this moonless night in the fading light. Darkness is our compass. Hurry—It is our time. It is now that the world belongs to us."

In a grand finale, there is a rush of sound and flight from within the closing darkness.

Then all is silent once more. The concert is over. The hunt is on.

And I am in awe—changed forever—still listening to the classical music of the forest.

Mimzi Schradi

"IF MUSIC BE THE FOOD OF LOVE, PLAY ON..." *

Sunday afternoon on Camano Island, I rush around in my tiny gourmet kitchen, preparing an ethnic meal for company. Feeling the need to relax, I pause, let out a deep breath, and become mesmerized by a familiar Hungarian melody from the past, now playing in the background on my Bose radio. All at once, I picture a bright red and white kitchen in an old Dutch Colonial home in Highland Park, New Jersey. A vision of myself as a child, helping my mother to prepare our Sunday feast comes into focus.

My mother stands up tall after placing all the multi-colored bowls, wooden spoons, and ingredients for our meal, on the kitchen table. She brushes the hair out of her face and wipes the sweat from her brow with an old, tattered cloth napkin she has tucked in her apron. I notice her weathered hands, which contrast with the red nail polish on her fingernails. As I put on my own small apron and ready myself to join her in the preparation of our Sunday company dinner, my eyes widen as she holds up a knife and an onion—a large, dried out relic from our garden. First, she peels the yellow husky globe of its outer core, revealing the white, shiny, pungent inside. With tears in her eyes, she smiles at me, then places the onion, like an unfinished work of art upon her cutting board. She looks at it for a moment then begins tearing it apart with her carving knife.

tune, *Three Blind Mice,* comes into my mind and haunts me. I wince, not from the odor of the onion, but from the image of mice tails being whacked to bits. But what do I know? I am only seven and my task alongside my mother is relegated to slicing cucumbers within the confines of a grater. After I peel and grate the cucumbers for the Hungarian Cucumber Salad—*Tejfeles uborka-salata,* I watch while my mother works as the master chef preparing *Toltott Kaposzta*—Stuffed Cabbage.

I study her as she plays the artist in our kitchen. She hums and sings along in her native tongue to the music playing on the *Hungarian Hour,* which airs every Sunday at noon on WOR, the local radio station. I recognize the tunes but cannot pronounce the words. I stare at her hands as they move in rhythm with the music while tossing a few sliced onions into my small red bowl.

I smile as my mother, Anna, coos to me, "Squeeze the cucumbers and onions until there is no liquid left in them, *kedves.* After that, put them in the blue bowl. Then you can add your vinegar, but not too much, and some sugar, a pinch of salt and pepper and don't forget the paprika."

I comply, but at the same time I keep watch on her as she continues preparing the main course. First, she mixes her chopped onions in the large yellow bowl with the cooked rice and raw chopped pork and beef that looks blood red to me. Not a pretty sight to a seven-year-old. Scary almost. Then she adds salt, pepper, dill and paprika.

"Come, my little Mimzi; try mixing this for me a little while. I have to take the cabbage out of the pot; it is boiling over. Do this for me, *kedves*."

So, I squeeze the mixture together like a potter mixing clay and the raw red meat no longer scares me. I mimic my mother—the professional gourmet in our kitchen—and enjoy the smells, and the textures I am creating. Enthralled with the process, I too, become the artist. I don't mind that the mixture is sticking to my hands, elbows, and arms.

"Now," my mother announces like the grand chef she is, "wash your hands and go finish preparing your salad. Then, when you are done, come back and watch me as I roll the cabbages."

I lean over the sink, soap, and rinse my hands, after scrapping the meat off my fingers with a washcloth, and then dry them on an old flour sack.

Returning to my station, I notice that a dollop of sour cream has been placed in my cucumber salad bowl. I take the thin wooden spoon lying next to it and mix up the salad delight, which is one of my favorites. I sprinkle it with paprika and hold it up for my mother to admire.

She smiles. "It's good, Mimzi." She tastes a bit with a spoon. "Perfect. Put some sliced red and green peppers on top and you will have the colors of the *Magyar* flag."

I smile and slice a few peppers with my grate and finish off my creation. I am beside myself with pride. My mother beams, delighted with my creation. "Now put it in the icebox and come watch me."

Opening the refrigerator door, I see some pigs' feet in a jelly-like kind of covering. "Ugg," I mutter quietly. Nestled in their plates, they remind me of the jelly fish I see washed ashore at the beach. After cringing a bit, I put the covered salad next to that detested delicacy only a full-blooded Hungarian could love, and return to stand alongside my mother, who has been making stuffed cabbage since before my brothers and I were born. I watch as she dries her hands on her floral printed apron, which is patched in numerous places, and has permanent stains no amount of detergent will remove.

First my mother pulls the cabbage out of the pot with a large fork and her carving knife, one leaf at a time and places a few on the cutting board. Then she takes a spoonful of her meaty delight and fills each one. She folds each cabbage leaf with her thumb and fingers, then rolls it over, tucking the last part inward and begins again, continuing the process until all the leaves are off the cabbage, filled and folded into rolls.

The cabbage rolls are nestled on the wooden board like little babies smiling at me. I chuckle as my mother tenderly places them together on a bed of chopped cabbage and sauerkraut to rest in the giant cast iron pot. After she layers them, she covers them with tomato sauce, dill, and a little water—a blanket of moisture to protect her precious creations from falling apart or drying out. She sets the pot, filled with the cabbage rolls and with its lid slightly ajar, on the stove to simmer. Soon the entire downstairs will be engulfed in a mouth-watering familiar aroma.

She turns to me. "Next time, you will help me roll out the cabbages. We have one hour to wait until dinner is done. All that needs to be done is to mash the potatoes. I'll do that, after the potatoes are done boiling. You can set the table in the dining room. We have fresh rye bread from the bakery, but don't put that out yet; it will get stale if we take it out too soon. But you can put the butter on the table, and the napkins—use the cloth ones, as it's Sunday. When you are done, you can practice your piano. Your brothers are upstairs; they won't bother you. Oh, I still have to make the *rantash* sauce. Go now. I will listen to you play as I prepare the *rantash szósz* for the cabbages."

I smile up at her and hug her around her waist. I can detect the smell of powder, rouge, and lipstick through the sweet kitchen odors. She pats my back,

kisses me gently and smiles back with a wink from her twinkling eyes.

"Thanks, Mommy!" Delighted I am free from cleaning up the dishes, pots, and pans, I pick up the butter dish and scurry out of the kitchen, thinking, *Anna always lets me off kitchen patrol early, if I play the piano.*

"Hurry up now. And play my favorite *Czárdás* for me."

"I will."

"I love when you play that piece…"

In a flash, holding the butter dish tight, I skip into our dining room. Setting the butter on the table, I remove the plates from the china closet and place them on the table. One of the plates is chipped. I put that in my spot. I take the white linen napkins out of the drawer and the silverware we only use on Sundays. After arranging them the best I can, I hurry into our small living room, which is dwarfed by an enormous upright piano.

After twirling the round piano stool to a comfortable height, I sit down at the ancient instrument and place my small fingers on the keys. I begin to pound out the melody with great ceremony—playing the old *Czárdás* melody that has been heard throughout the ages. I play with much flare, albeit a few wrong notes. And while I play for myself, I also play for my mother, experiencing the joy, the connection between us through this music and through our cooking together. It is a heavenly feeling. I hear my mother's voice drifting in my direction over the pounding of my fingers on the keys.

"Lovely, my dear, beautiful."

Years later and thousands of miles away in my home in the state of Washington, I am the chef, preparing a Sunday dinner for company. As I set the table, placing a bottle of wine in the center, next to the rye bread and cucumber salad, I continue to hear that familiar *Czárdás* in my head, and realize that its chords and melody are like the peeling of an onion. No matter how many times I hear it; no matter how many times I play it, I only have to peel off the layers of the melody and my past comes back to me. And, unexpectedly, without warning, its scent grabs me, the tears begin to fall, and I am back in my childhood home, safe in my mother's love.

*Quote from Twelfth Night, Act I scene I, A Comedy by William Shakespeare

Stuffed Cabbage (*Toltott Kaposzta*)

½ lb. ground beef
½ lb. ground pork
2 tsp. salt
1 tsp. paprika
½ tsp. black pepper
½ cup rice
1 egg
1 large onion
2 tbsp. lard or butter
1 large head cabbage—or two small heads

1 medium can tomato puree or sauce (may also add an addition can of diced tomatoes)
1 clove garlic (optional)
Dill for topping chopped slightly

(Ingredients may be doubled for a larger crowd.)

Place cored cabbage in boiling water. Cook. When slightly soft, hold cabbage in water firmly with fork. With knife, cut away leaves as they wilt and remove from water. Drain and put in meat mixture and roll up individual leaves. Hold leaf in one hand and place a tablespoonful of meat mixture in leaf. Hold leaf and with other hand, fold one side of leaf over mixture and roll. Tuck in other end of leaf gently but firmly. Place a layer of chopped cabbage on bottom of large pot, then water to cover. Add a clove of garlic. After tomato sauce has been added, sprinkle with dill weed. Cook over low flame for about one hour or until the rice and meat are cooked. Add gravy (below).

Gravy *(Rantash szósz)*

1 tbsp. butter
In frying pan melt butter, add flour slowly,
2 tbsp. flour stirring mixture.
Fry slowly until mixture browns
½ tsp. paprika
Add paprika and stir until lumps disappear. Add to cooked stuffed cabbage.
Cucumber Salad (*Tejfeles uborka-sala'ta*)
2 large cucumbers
2 tbsp. vinegar
¼ tsp. black pepper
¼ tsp. paprika
1 clove garlic—chopped
1 small onion—minced
1 tbsp. salt
1 cup sour cream

Peel and slice cucumbers in thin round slices. A food processor works well. Put into a medium-sized bowl. Sprinkle with salt and let stand for about ½ hour. Squeeze out excess moisture. Place in serving bowl and add seasoning, vinegar, and sour cream. Mix well and serve with meat, fish, or fowl. The recipe may be doubled or tripled as needed for number of guests.

Mimzi Schradi

WALKING ON THE BEACH WITH JARED

I pause to feel the wind on my face and gaze at the surf,
calm for a rainy day
The dogs tug at my heel, wrapping me up like a present
with their leashes
Jared interrupts my dilemma and reaches up to me with
his small hands.

"Here's some rope, Mimi, I found just for you."
Sidetracked by the dogs, I look at the sandy wet yellow
rope, twisted, knotted, and torn

"It's all sandy, Sweetheart, and I have no pockets and
no hands to hold it…"

Jared drops the rope as I untangle myself and we walk
on
But the yellow rope tugs at my heart
We head home under darkening clouds
A new storm approaches

The wind blows sand into our eyes and hurries us off
the beach.

The next morning, I rise early, before the others
At six a.m. I return to the sandy shore
It is the calm after the storm
I walk in silence, feeling the salty air in my pores, and
listen to the steady roar of the receding surf...

I am alone in my thoughts, with Misty and Bear, my
furry friends, my only companions besides the seagulls,
following behind me
In search of the twisted, yellow rope.
Despite wind and tide, the remnant remains,
miraculously by the side of the dune
Right where my youngest grandson dropped it.
I pick up the tattered remnant like it is buried treasure
Wipe some sand off on my sweatshirt.
And tuck the tattered, sandy rope into my pocket for
safekeeping.
I take Jared's gift home, rinse off the remaining sand in
the sink
And display my special present in a place of honor on
my dresser.

Later, over breakfast I tell Jared how much I love the
golden piece of rope
He found for me the day before
And I say to myself, "I will cherish it forever."

ABOUT THE AUTHOR

Mimzi Schradi interweaves life experience and imagination into her writing, adding color and texture through her travels, love of nature and participation in the arts. Her family, friends and her Cairn Terrier help create the inner peace that surrounds her writing. Her published works include two books in the Angelina Seraphina Series—PsyChic in Seattle, and Frantic in Fiji...and other ports of call, and a third one (Poisoned in Paris) soon to be released. She has written a novella in the e-book collaboration called Detective Ink with the "Prime Five Authors." Poetry of hers is also published in Tales for a Lazy Afternoon, an Anthology by the Skagit Valley Writers League. She also has won poetry and creative non-fiction awards for her work in the new Skagit River Anthology.

Gloria Two-Feathers

SONS OF THE WIND

There is a circle in me, dwelling within my heart
In dawn's early light, I rise with the Sun, Father of the
Sky
Bathing myself in light, igniting my soul

Despair, Birther of Hope, grateful seeing
Nurturing mystery gives me a familiar form
What future self, resides in me

Wind of the East, Fire, Birther of Mornings, Seeker of
Visions,
Truth Teller, Bell Ringer, Bringer of Smoke, Unknown
Singer,
Voice of Inner Being emerges from the flame
I circle around

Wind of the South, Earth, Planter of Seeds,
Scent of Love, Eternal Hope, Dreamer, Re-Birther
Old worn-out habits no longer serve

100

I circle around

Wind of the West, Water, Healer, Storyteller,
Servant of Time, where all days' have gone
Ancestors announce my place in line
I circle around

Wind of the North, Air, Warrior of Thought,
Wisdom, standing tall, fully grown
Diviner wearing foolishness
I circle around the boundaries of the Earth

In the Center of the Hoop, opposites interact
Where all roads meet is a Holy Place
I circle around on open wings I fly

Sons of Balance
Sons of Eternity
Sons of the Circle
Sons of the Wind blow eternally

Gloria Two-Feathers

THE MISSING MOON

Ancient Grandmother Moon lived high in the sky with the stars. For eons, her silvery light bathed the Earth Mother. Those who lived on the Earth considered hers to be the most beautiful of all light.

The Earth endlessly turned, Grandmother Moon kept track of time, showing her face in many phases from a small sliver to her full faced brightness, and back to a sharp sickle.

It was known at the beginning of her new cycle there would be temporary darkness. During these three nights she would put on a black robe. Pulling the hood over her long silvery tresses, she turned her face away to look at the heavens. At this time of darkness all creatures would rest.

As Grandmother Moon journeyed across Earth Mother, she looked down and noticed a dense gloomy forest that even her full faced radiance did not penetrate. When she was looking away during her dark time, she heard sounds of terror and suffering coming from that place.

Grandmother Moon loved all the creatures below and this deeply concerned her. She was worried and decided, *"On my next dark cycle I will descend to the Earth and see for myself what could possibly be causing this distress. What, or who, could be so cruel as to create this suffering?"*

Putting on her black robes she began her descent, sliding all the way through a low-lying cloud. She landed as softly as a beam of her light on the ground at the edge of the dark forest.

Even though she held her robes close to her body, and the hood tied tight around her shining silver strands of hair, her radiance could never be completely covered. The tiniest sliver of light shone around her beautiful face. With each step she took, as she entered the dark place, a dim aura peaked out under the hem.

As far as she could see, broken and sharp jagged trees stuck up out of a swamp. In places the swamp had turned into great black bogs. Rotting plants filled the darkness with the scent of decay. Black slimy muck was everywhere. An unearthly silence hung in the air.

Grandmother Moon felt an ominous presence.

"I have not felt this since the time when the old monsters dwelled on Earth. Evil lives here."

Nevertheless, the love she felt for all creatures was stronger than her fear of this dark lightless place.

Slowly putting one foot in-front of the other, she walked deeper into the dark forest.

The solid path between the bogs was narrow and slippery. In the deep darkness she had to feel her way through tangled old roots and dying plants.

Something cold slithered up over the top of her bare foot. She stumbled back, her robes parting enough that pale silver light shown on the large root reaching toward her. She twisted away but lost her balance, with a great Sploosh, fell into the dark and slimy bog. As dying plants wrapped themselves greedily around her, pulling her deeper into the black muck, she realized, too late, what was happening.

"The dead and dying trees are under the control of the Evil Ones!"

She fought and struggled with all her might, but the plants pulled her deeper into the black depth. Exhausted she lay buried in the mud, quietly straining against her bindings with her fading strength. The muffled laughter of the Evil Ones grew louder. Then out of the darkness came a splash and a loud screech, followed by pathetic whimpering. Tears of helplessness ran like rivers down her silver face. With a great effort Grandmother Moon raised her head. In the dim light escaping from under her hood, she could make out the shape of a raccoon, its eyes wide with fright, stuck in the muck struggling for its life.

Grandmother Moon realized the raccoon had seen the dim aura escaping out of her robe.

"The poor animal thought my light would lead it out of the dark forest. But I lured it deeper into danger and possibly to its own death."

Grandmother Moon called upon the last of her strength. Renewing her struggle, she managed to slightly slip her hood away from her beautiful face. One slender strand of silver hair slipped free. A dazzling beam of her powerful light radiated into the darkness.

The raccoon looked up at a sturdy branch just above its head. Struggling free of the sucking bog, it reached up with both hand-like paws, grasped the branch, and heaved itself up and out of the black death. It scrambled down the tree trunk and then with a great leap, landed on the solid ground of the path and ran out of the dark forest. Never once did it look back to see the source of light that saved its life.

Exhausted by her struggle to help the raccoon, Grandmother Moon slumped back, her hood falling back over her glowing hair. All was once again dark, and once again she was alone. But at least the raccoon had escaped. Her strength gone, she gave up resisting and slowly sank further into the quagmire.

As she sank, she heard the laughter of those Ones that loved and lived in the putrid dark. She heard their whispers as the bog slowly filled her ears.

"Now we shall bury you. No one will ever find you. Now the time of light will end. And the darkness will grow."

They jumped in glee on her, pushing her deeper and deeper down under the black sucking mud. There was a shriek of triumph as the Evil Ones rolled a large boulder over the place the Grandmother Moon lay buried in the black oozy muck.

A darkness came upon the land. Looking across the sky, the Sun missed his nighttime companion. In his grief he covered his face with clouds.

Weeping, his tears rained down like falling stars on the Earth. Without Grandmother Moon to reflect his light, the Sun's brilliance was dimmed during the day. Without his warmth the days were dark and cold.

Without Grandmother Moon's loving light showing down from the night sky to guide them, the animals no longer went out to the meadows and fields to eat. It was so dark it was difficult for even the owls and bats to fly.

The fish in the rivers could no longer see to navigate the rapids and boulders. Without her to draw the tides, the oceans no longer went in and out. The sea creatures lost their direction and didn't know up from down.

As Grandmother Moon lay in the tomb of muck she pleaded in a muffled voice.

"Help, Help me!"

The Evil Ones danced around the boulder in triumph, taunting her. "No one can hear you. No one will come into our dark bog to help you!"

Grandmother Moon thought of those she loved and watched over for countless centuries. She longed to see their dreaming faces again as they looked up at her. She thought of her companion the Sun and the way they look at each other, across the heavens. She remembered how he would shine his warmth on her, lighting her face. *"Will I ever see him and share the sky with him again?"*

Grandmother Moon took all her weakened life force and turned it inward enforcing her power of the dream time and her magnetic force of drawing others to her. The faintest soft silvery blue light emanated around the bottom edge of the heavy boulder.

The animals dreamed.

The Evil Ones have captured Grandmother Moon.

The fish stirred in the dark waters.

The Evil Ones intended to keep her.

The birds shifted on their cold roosts.

The Evil Ones have stolen her light from the world.

All awoke to a strange urge to go out into the dark night. An undeniable force drew them to the meadow at the edge of the dark forest.

They stood in the never-ending darkness. A raven flew in carrying a flaming branch and placed it on top of a large rock. In the small flickering light, they formed a circle.

They began talking all at once. Grunting, huffing, howling, yipping, squeaking, honking, chirping, and hooting filled the meadow.

"What has happened to Grandmother Moon?"

"Has anyone seen her?"

"Where can she be?"

"We cannot live without her."

Wise Owl hooted loudly to silence them. "One at a time."

Eagle hopped forward and spread her great wings wide, yellow eyes glowing in the firelight, "I have flown above the clouds and over the mountain tops. So high I could see the curve of Mother Earth. I flew in all directions, and I can tell you she's not in the sky."

Bear stood up to his full height, huffing. "I have looked in all the caves. There is only darkness. She is not there."

Sitting up on her back legs, graceful tail wrapped around her feet, Otter said, "I have swum the dark rivers, lakes, and oceans. Her light is not there."

Elk, Moose, Deer, and Ram all agreed they could not find her in the mountains.

Buffalo and Wolf said, "She is not on the prairie."

All the birds, mice, and squirrels chirped, crowed, tweeted, and squeaked. "We could not find her in the grass or trees."

Suddenly, Bat, with folded wings, took an awkward step forward. Her sharp pointed ears stood straight up. "Do you hear that?"

They listened intently, heads cocked and ears straining for any sound. And right at that moment, a slight breath of wind carried faint and eerie laughter to them. They looked towards the dark forest.

Many of them cowered close to the ground. Some snarled, white teeth gleaming in the fire light. Others stood tall, heads up, peering into the darkness. All of them were leery of the dark smelly place. Many had loved ones who had gone in and had never been seen again.

"Grandmother Moon lights our path at night. She reveals any danger and guides us on our hunts. All mothers nurse and take care of our young in her soft light. She cares for us. It's only right that we help her," stated Mother Wolf.

They agreed they had to do something.

Frog and Toad hopped and leaped forward. "We have been in the bog before. We will go in to see if Grandmother Moon is there."

Deep in the dark forest in the middle of the bog they found a huge boulder. In guttural croaks they consulted each other.

"Where did this come from?"

"I don't remember it being here before. We must tell the others."

Following the dim point of light made by the burning branch, they hasten out of the foreboding place and hopped up to the waiting group.

"We came upon a big boulder. We don't remember it being there before," Toad said in a deep croak.

Frog leaped excitedly. "There was a faint glow around the bottom of it."

Everyone wanted to help despite their fear and so it was decided they would go together into the ominous dark place. On silent wings, Owl led the way. The darkness was so deep even with his great eyes, he could barely see.

The Lightning Bugs did their best to light the foul-smelling air. Raven flew behind them carrying the fire branch, so the others could see the narrow strip of solid ground and prevent them from falling into the black mire.

Bats fluttered overhead diving into the great swarms of mosquitoes and flying insects that bit, stung, stinging, and crawled into the eyes, noses, and ears of the rescue group.

Wolf, with her nose to the ground, picked up the faint scent of Grandmother Moon and howled with excitement, "She has been here. We are on the right trail."

When they arrived at the huge boulder in the middle of the muck there was the tiniest line of silvery light emanating out of the bottom edge. A faint call for help came from below. In the light of Raven's fire branch, they could see a wink of a red eye and the flash of a claw as the Evil Ones slithered, splish-splashing, withdrawing further back into the darkness.

Crow, with the help of the smaller birds, came flying in with long twisted vines. Grabbing the ends of the vines, mouse and squirrel leaped onto the top of the boulder and tied the ends securely around it. Then they tied the other ends around the necks of the big birds. With a whoosh of wings, their necks strained straight out, Herons, Cranes, and Geese rose pulling with all their might on the heavy stone. It did not budge. Honking, squawking, and chirping encouragement they tried again and again. The heavy rock did not move.

Ram lowered his hard head and ran smack into one of the black gnarled trees. Down it went, to lay between the path and the boulder. Bear, standing on his back legs, placed his huge paws against another tree, and with a loud crack, pushed it down. Again, and again they knocked tree after tree down, creating a bridge.

Beaver hastily covered the broken trees with black oozy mud and whacked and slapped it into the cracks with his broad flat tail. In the light and heat of Raven's fire branch it quickly dried to a hard surface.

Elk, Moose, and Stag Deer ran across the bridge. Using their large racks of horns, they pried at the boulder. Wolf, Bear, and Buffalo stayed on the path. Buffalo, with a twisted vine wrapped around his horns, planted his hooves firmly on the narrow path. He lowered his massive head and heaved his great weight, pulling the boulder. Wolf, grasping the end of a vine in her teeth, backed up, lurching, and pulling with all her strength. Bear grasped a vine in his strong jaws, sharp claws dug into the narrow path straining his broad shoulder muscles.

Geese, Cranes, and Herron flapped their large strong wings.

Coyote yipped and cried, "All together, pry, push, pull, fly! Again, all together! Now! Again!

Owl, with his large clear eyes, saw the tiny crack of light widen. "Don't stop! It's moving!"

Coyote yipped, "Again all together!

Suddenly, with a deafening, earsplitting sucking sound, the large boulder gave up its seal in the inky muck and rolled over. All the animals looked down into the deepest, darkest pit they had ever seen. At the bottom they saw the beautiful ancient face of their beloved Grandmother Moon. The mice and squirrels scurried down into the pit, using their sharp teeth, they gnawed the roots apart and the vines slipped away.

Opening her old eyes, she began to rise.

Owl on silent wings and Heron with delicate neck folded back took to the air escorting their old beautiful loved one as she rose higher and higher.

The wind sighed softly with relief, making the trees sway gently as they briefly held Grandmother Moon in their branches. She lifted higher, pausing to kiss the mountain peaks as they, too momentarily cradled her.

The higher she rose the brighter she became. Silver light radiated out through the dark forest, leaving only shadows. Her illuminated light shown across land and water.

She looked back to those who had risked their lives to rescue her with bright love in her eyes. The other side of her face looked to the heavens. Comets arched as they shot across the sky. Just beyond the light of the stars, the Great Mystery sang a song that had not been heard since the time of creation. Grandmother Moon continued to rise until she once again sat in her appointed place high above Mother Earth.

When the animals could no longer see her eyes in her beautiful face they ran on the narrow path, out of the shadowed forest into the moonlit meadow. In joy and happiness, they rolled, leaped, jumped, swooped, hopped, howled, and played in the light of Grandmother Moon.

That night Grandmother Moon once again sent a dream to all of them at once.

"I promise. I will never leave you again."

As the morning dawned, the horizon glowed with radiating pink light, coloring the clouds. The Sun rose bright and warm, sending out yellow beams of light.

All of creation sighed with relief, as if it had been holding its breath.

Grandmother Moon felt and received the love of those who rescued her. Her light now shown brighter than it had before. Grandmother Moon continues moving through her phases, marking time because her radiance cannot be contained. Now during her dark time, when she dons her black hooded robes, they appear grey. On the three nights of her renewal, all can look up and see she is still there, keeping her promise.

You may wonder what happened to the Evil Ones, and the dark forest with its mucky, smelly bog. Yes, they are still there. Grandmother Moon understands the Earth Mother loves all she has created and doesn't choose between her children. The Earth Mother for her own reasons, keeps the dark places and the Evil Ones who live there.

But now Grandmother Moon's light penetrates even the darkest places, giving hope and guidance to those who choose to venture within and walk the narrow paths.

Gloria Two-Feathers

WHAT IS IN A NAME

To know what is in the name of the Earth
I pressed my face to the ground and laid in
the mystery of grass beginning

I moved in a circle until I discovered an ant,
its heart full of knowledge
Now we have something in common
A point of view in a world that is larger than us

With an Eagle's vision, I looked at the leaf of a
newborn tree and discovered a universe

Drifting on clouds I looked down at my small life
The path strewn with stones of my old mistakes,
so sharp they cut my knees to the bone and flowers,
scented so sweet they made me weep

Exciting unpredictable wild card called Life
In the great continuation, Earth teaches me
What is in her name

Gloria Two-Feathers

SACRED MESSENGER

Rain and drought have a rhythm. But during the times of drought there is always a seed that is held by something or someone for a future generation.

I was experiencing my personal drought when I met Buck, a Native American elder. And a lot of the rain came in the form of a sacred ceremony called a Sweat Lodge.

Buck was Sicangu Lakota from South Dakota. He stood five foot four inches tall, weighed 135 pounds soaking wet, and had long black braids down to the middle of his back. His charismatic, humorous personality was contagious. He had a light in his eyes, and he carried a large spirit. Buck was one of the wisest and biggest men I will ever know. I didn't know when I first met him that he was to become my Spiritual Elder and Uncle.

Did you ever have a time in your youth when you thought you knew everything? And then one day you wake up and take a good look around and you're

116

not sure who you are or where your place is in the world. I was in that place in my life. I felt like the earth was crumbling under my feet and I didn't know what to do to save myself.

My young daughter and I had recently moved from the South Dakota, Wyoming area to the Pacific Northwest. I left all my family and friends so I could begin a new life in a new place. This new life all alone without family wasn't as easy to live as I thought it would be.

We had lived in the Seattle area just a short time when I received the sad news my elderly father had crossed over to the Spirit World. My father was my only parent, and I didn't know how I would handle this new life without his strength, guidance, and wisdom to help and guide me.

Within a year of my father's passing, my young daughter began running away and living on the streets; of course, drugs and alcohol were involved. And all the other things that kind of lifestyle involves.

The reality of my life seemed so much bigger than me. I didn't know who to turn to or what to do. I was being crushed under the enormous weight of it.

I had been attending weekly classes Uncle Buck taught in his home. One night after class I was relating my circumstances to him, asking for any wisdom he may have to share with me.

"Niece," he said. "I can't help you heal, but I can help you find that healing place within yourself. You need to get into a Sweat Lodge and pray. We're having one this weekend. You will need to wear a plain skirt with leggings and a tee shirt. Don't forget to bring a towel."

I had never been to a Sweat Lodge, and I wasn't sure what to expect. I was feeling excited and anxious as I gathered my things in preparation to go. As I left my apartment and walked to my car, I heard a distant whistle above me. Looking up into the sky I saw an eagle soaring in a circle. I knew Eagle was a messenger of the Great Spirit. A rush of goose bumps flash through my body.

When I arrived, there was a large group of men and women preparing to go into the Lodge. Uncle was with two men, one the fire tender and one the singer.

The Sweat Lodge itself was constructed of saplings inserted into the ground forming a circle. They were bent over and tied together, creating a low dome structure resembling the shape of a turtle shell. It was fully covered with several layers of blankets to create a dark space inside. The low east-facing door had a flat-topped earthen altar in front of it. A few feet away on the east side of the altar was a large fire heating several cantaloupe sized stones.

As Uncle taught us in class. The ancient Stone Lodge Ceremony is the oldest ceremony known to mankind. It is conducted in four rounds and is based upon the six directions. The Spirit above, the Earth below, and the four cardinal directions West, North, East, and South; these four archetypal Spirits are known to be the helpers of the Great Spirit. Each one carries a specific energy.

I can still hear Uncle saying, the West is the place where we come from, and we go back to. It's the place of our Ancestor's live in the ever-present Spirit World. This is where we go to heal and it's the place of the life-giving rains.

The North is the source of endurance, strength, truthfulness, and honesty.

The East is the place of the sunrise, knowledge, and meditation. Without knowledge, we can harm ourselves and maybe others.

The South is the place of rebirth, medicine, love, and growth.

Before entering the Lodge, asked me to stand at the door facing the West, raise my hands to the sky and turn in a slow, clockwise circle, acknowledging each direction as I turned. I repeated his words as he said them, saying, *'Aho Mitakuye Oyasin,'* meaning All My Relations. To enter through the low door, I had to get down on your hands and knees, humbling myself, as I entered the womb of the Earth Mother.

Uncle instructed me to crawl around the stone pit in the center and sit in the West facing the door in the East. The others entered, seating themselves in setting in a circle around the stone pit. Uncle and his singer sat on each side of the open door.

"Fire Tender, Uncle said. Seven stones!"

One by one the Fire Tender bought red-hot stones on a pitchfork and placed them into the stone pit. The hot stones had a wonderful, sweet smell, unlike anything I had ever smelled before.

After the seven stones had been placed in the pit, Uncle spoke. "Fire Tender bring the darkness."

The door flap was bought down, and it was so dark I couldn't see my hand in front of my face. Uncle placed some dried herbs on the hot stones. I could see them glow brightly before they disintegrated.

The Lodge filled with a sweet fragrance that swirled around my body. I breathed it in. He poured ladles of water on the stones, creating steam that mingled with the herbs.

"The steam from the stones, mixed with the plants, become powerful medicine. We purify our bodies by sweating out the toxins of disease," Uncle said. Together they provide balance, soothe troubled emotions, and help you come back into your center."

Buck explained that we are connected to everything on the Earth through the Great Spirit. So, we must pray for all that is. He sent the prayer around the circle asking each person in turn to speak. Prayers were said for the trees, for the water, for the earth, for the wind, for the sun and moon, and stars. Prayers were spoken for stones, plants, for the winged, the four legged, the swimmers, and the creepy crawlies, and finally for the elders, the children, the mothers and fathers, and the warriors who kept us safe.

After the prayers, we heard Uncle's voice in the darkness. "Each of you crawled into what seemed like a very small space. But if you look around you, you will see there are no boundaries or limits here. You are sitting in the middle of the Universe and all its creations. This is the place of full potential." He called for a prayer song, and our voices joined the singer as he began to beat his drum to the rhythm of a heartbeat.

When we finished singing, Uncle called out. "Fire Tender bring the light!"

The flap opened and light poured in, shining on the darkness of our ignorance. We had finished our first round. More hot stones were bought in, the door closed, and the same was continued for three more rounds.

As I sat in the Lodge praying and singing, I noticed the space around me filling with a presence I could only describe as something that was bigger than me or my suffering. I was being touched by the Great Spirit. I began to feel this presence inside of me. I was experiencing sacred grace. I felt the life-giving rain returning to me after a very long drought. It was nourishing and bringing that seed deep inside of me to life.

I returned to the Lodge every week. Uncle's teachings were showing me how to be a good human being and how to live as a strong respectful woman. I came to understand the honor and dignity the Great Spirt bestowed on all womankind and of the important and responsible role women have as the carriers of life. I discovered what my original medicine was, that I was a healer and a teacher. I was finding my place in the world.

Each Lodge followed the same steps but each one was a different experience. Quite often Uncle would tell stories in the Lodge. Some of these were creation stories that are so old no one remembered how old they were. These stories helped our ancestors understand the Great Incomprehensible Mystery. I especially loved the ones that were first told by the Grandmother Spirits and past down to the people.

One of my favorite stories was about a Sacred Messenger.

Because time often folds into itself, no one knew when she was born. But all agreed, it was sometime between the beginning and the end of the world. Most importantly the Memory Keepers said they knew where she was born.

Tate the Wind remembered he blew as a gentle breeze that day, warmed by Wi the Sun.

He moved through the Standing Nation, swaying their branches, and rustling their leaves, ahshooow, ahshooow, ahshooow. The plants and grass heard and began whispering, whirr, whirr, whirr.

Tate breathed over the face of Ma-hne, the Water, and she began to sing her song of gurgling and tinkling. He carried a sacred message, "It's time, she is arriving!" And nature sang a song of welcoming. Tate continued his journey deep, deep into the heart of the Old Forest.

There on the soft, fragrant green needles, under the protective boughs of the Great Grandmother Tree, she lay nestled next to her mother's warm body, in the graceful curve of her long legs. Wi the Sun's warm light was shining through the branches creating spots on her smooth damp fur. Tate tenderly breathed Niya, the first breath of life, into her lungs and caressed her, parting the hair on her forehead, the first breath created a pattern that looked like a cedar leaf. This mark remained for all her life.

Everyone knew she was different. She grew a little faster and a little larger; her deep golden-tan fur was radiant with an inner glow; her legs were longer, and she moved more gracefully than the others. All of nature loved her

It was during the time her spots faded, on a warm Indian Summer Day, that she had the dream. Bright yellow and fire-red colored leaves fell around her as she lay resting; the air had a *crisp smell. In the dream-world it seemed like a moment ago; it was the time just before her birth that she stood in the presence of the Creator. He asked if she would be one of his helpers, be a Sacred Messenger to those who had lost their way on Maka, Mother Earth.*

She woke from the dream with a special spirit light in her eyes as she remembered her life's purpose. Quickly she rose, moving so gracefully through the forest it appeared as though her feet didn't touch the ground. Those who gazed upon her recognized she was different. They were seeing her for who she really was: Wakan, a Sacred BWith her large, velvety ears rotating she sensed a distant sound that was carried on Tate the Wind. She felt the call and followed the faint sound deep into the heart of the old forest to the Great Grandmother Tree, the place of her birth.

In the lengthening shadows and the fading light, standing in a soft glow was a beautiful woman. This woman was Wophe, the daughter of the Great Spirit. She could sense Wophe's powerful energy of beauty, friendship, compassion, and happiness.

As she stepped into the glowing aura, Wophe reached out and touched the cedar leaf pattern on her forehead, transferring some of her own energy qualities to her. Speaking quietly, stroking the large delicate ears, Wophe said, "By using the gift of listening you will be able to hear the questions in the troubled hearts of those who have lost their way. By focusing on one heart at a time, you can appear magically before that person. When they see you, their

*hearts will open and their confusion will clear, so
they receive the answer to their prayers." At that
moment, the Spirit Deer began to listen. She is
still listening to this very day.*

I continued to go to the weekly Sweat Lodges
and the weeks turned into years. One day Uncle pulled
me aside. "Niece, it is time for you to learn how to pour
a Lodge."

It took me several more years to learn how to
conduct this ceremony so it wouldn't harm anyone and
to understand how to serve the people in this way. But
the day did come when I built a Lodge on my land. I
started to pour monthly Lodges for those who wanted to
come and pray.

My life turned around. I married my best friend of
many years, and our marriage was strong loving. I had
my own healing practice, and I began to teach others.
This led me to open a school of Energy Medicine.
Establishing this new field of education was very
rewarding, while full of challenges and countless hours.
I loved my school, the students, and the material that
was being taught.

Some of my old challenges persisted. I
continued to have relationship issues with my daughter
and one of my sons. Both were involved in drugs and
alcohol. This bought a dysfunctional lifestyle to my
grandchildren. But I kept trying to help all of them. No
matter what challenges life threw at me.

I still had my Sweat Lodge, the one place where
I could go to cleanse, pray, and receive guidance from
the Great Spirit. In the second half of my life, I
experienced loss when my two older brothers and a
close friend died. I was entering another time of drought
and as I was aging Uncle was getting older, one day the

phone rang, and I received the news Uncle had suddenly and unexpectedly died of a heart attack. I was devastated. But I held his teachings and continued to share them with others as I poured Lodges.

Despite all effort my family completely fell apart. I could feel and hear my heart breaking when I accepted the fact, I could not save my adult children from the decisions they had made.

At the same time the world economy entered a financial recession, leading to losing my school's student loan program. After a couple of years, I had to close its doors. I found myself unemployed for the first time in my life. Within days of closing my school, my beloved sister was diagnosed with terminal cancer; nine weeks after her diagnosis she crossed over into the Spirit World.

I was filled with grief; I didn't know how much more I could bear. I was under so much stress I wasn't surprised that I became ill and had to have emergency surgery. To make matters worse due to me being unemployed we had lost our health insurance. Between the financial burden of closing my school and the medical bills we were devastated. I felt completely lost and overwhelmed.

The winter of 2012 was one of the wettest winters on record. The heavy rains left the area where I built my Lodge under water through the winter and into the spring.

Then the adverse weather conditions persisted, bringing a hot and dry summer. Because of severe dry conditions there was a burn ban, and we could not build a fire to heat the sacred stones.

Between flooding and burn bans, I poured only one Lodge that entire year.

On a sizzling summer day, I sat on my back porch staring at the uncovered framework of my Lodge. With a heavy heart, I sent a prayer to the Great Spirit.

"Is this also something that is going away? Is this a sign that I should quit pouring Lodges? Should I take down my Lodge? Please let me know what you want me to do."

As I waited quietly, hoping for an answer to my prayer, a doe appeared, standing at the edge of the old growth cedar and fir trees on the west side of my Lodge area. As she moved forward, I saw she was she was special and realized she was Walking in a Sacred Manner. She crossed the open space to the Lodge, paused, and turning her long, graceful neck, and she looked at me. Then she went back into the West. She disappeared without making a sound. My heart beat rapidly. I drew in a deep breath. I was as alert as a jack rabbit that had seen something moving in the brush.

For a few minutes, all of nature became quiet; even the breeze was still, as if holding its breath. I felt an electrical charge in the hot air. Suddenly the doe appeared again out of the tall trees. With her beautiful head held high, the sun glinting off her golden hair, she walked to the north side of the Lodge. She sniffed all over the ribs of the open uncovered frame. Then her large brown eyes looked directly at me.

As she returned into the trees on the west side of the Lodge, everything in me said *pay attention!* A rush of goose bumps rippled my skin just like the moment, years ago, when Eagle circled above me. I knew something sacred was occurring. The charge of spirit energy filled me as I felt butterflies in my stomach and a rush of goose bumps rippled on my skin.

Out of the corner of my eye I noticed several ravens, who are the Gatekeepers between the worlds, quietly gathering in the high branches. A few dry leaves fell, and the shadows lengthened as the sun crossed the top of the trees. Then I saw her large ears as she silently moved through the dry grass on the south side of the Lodge area. I smelled the dust that stirred under her delicate black hooves when she walked into the clearing. Standing quietly in the sun, rotating her lovely black ears back and forth, she once again locked her soft brown eyes on me. Moments passed before she returned to the tall grass. The ravens began gliding to the lower branches to silently watch and wait, holding space for what was to come next.

She circled around to walk from the east to the Lodge. With great interest, she sniffed all over the benches and chairs where numerous people sit as they waited for the Lodge to begin. Stepping toward the fire pit, she continued her inspection of the burned, scorched ground and the ashes from previous fires. She sniffed all over the small, flat-topped earthen altar that sets in front of the door of the Lodge. Suddenly the ravens cawed in unison, sounding like a cackling chorus. With a loud caw, one of the ravens spread its black iridescent wings, and gliding silently, it came to rest on top of the Lodge, taking up a position of a lone sentinel.

The doe, bending onto her knees, lowered herself and crawled through the small door of the Lodge. Resting there with her head bowed, she appeared to be praying.

With the raven standing guard, she backed out of the door, rose, and met my astonished gaze. My whole being was focused on her soft sensitive face. In a heart-stopping moment, I entered the transcendent, timeless space when one experiences the divine. Her radiant brown eyes sent me a message of love and compassion. She may have looked at me for a few seconds or for a lifetime; I will never know. She circled around the Lodge and returned into the west where she had come from. Not a twig snapped, not a leaf rustled. She just disappeared.

For a long time, I stood looking up into the sky. Then I saw a cloud taking shape until it blotted out the sun, making shadows across my Lodge area. I called out thanking the Great Spirit. With an eagle feather in my hand, I danced the wild dances of my youth. I could smell the rain as a few drops fell into the dust of my dry land. My drought was over. The rain had come.

My eyes filled with tears of joy and wonder. My heart was full of gratitude for the Great Spirit, who had heard my prayers and touched my troubled heart. I felt humbled and awed with how He reached across time and space, to send me a Sacred Messenger, with the answer to my prayer.

As time continues to fold and unfold into itself, many worlds have begun, and many worlds have ended. However, this story is never ending.

People throughout time have told their own story of a beautiful Spirit Deer who appeared to them in the most peculiar place and time, seemingly out of nowhere. She appeared to be friendly and unafraid of them. As she moved gracefully, they saw compassion in her lovely, sensitive face and large expressive eyes. When she gazed at them, their troubled hearts calmed. They received an answer to their prayers.

More importantly, they felt the Great Spirit sent them a message through
the most beautiful of creatures, just when it was needed the most.
As it was then, so it is now. Ah ho!
Mitakuye Oyasin!

ABOUT THE AUTHOR

Gloria Two-Feathers coming from a unique Scottish and Native American heritage, hers was a family of storytellers, who used analogies, oral history, and jokes to teach her and her six siblings. From hunting, to canning, to the history of the family's South Dakota homestead, each topic came alive in the telling. As an adult Gloria adventured to Wyoming and then to the Seattle area. Having a huge impact on her life path, Lakota Elder, Buck Ghost Horse instructed her over a 20-year period about spirituality, ritual, ceremony, and culture — eventually giving Gloria her name. This connection to Native American culture resonated strongly with Gloria, reinforcing her sense that everything is alive. She brings this extraordinary sensibility to the stories and poems that have begun to flow through her in this newest chapter of her life.

Published Children's books:

Tallulah'sFlyingAdventure,2016   *Buck Keeper of the Meadow*, 2020.

Publications:

Sacred Messenger, 2014,

DivanintheMoon http://healingstory.org/publications/diving-in-the-moon-journal-2014/.

Awards:

Tallulah's Flying Adventure, 2018, 1st Place in CIBAs, Gertrude Warner, Middle Grade Reader.

The Missing Moon, 2021, Honorable Mention, Skagit Valley Writers League Literary Awards for Short Story Fiction

Poetry:

Sons of the Wind, 2021, Second place, Skagit Valley Writers League Literary Awards. Awards.

What is in a Name, Honorable Mention, Skagit Valley Writers League Literary Awards for Poetry.

Gloria's books can be purchased at Quest Books, Village Books and Paper Dreams, local bookstores, Libraries, and Ingram Sparks. Audio, eBook, and print books are available on Amazon.

Contact Information:

Email: gloria@gloriatwofeathers.com **Website:** www.gloriatwofeathers.comwww.sitkawriters.com

Naomi Wark

ALASKA YUKON PACIFIC EXPEDITION

Edna's sister was gone. In the weeks
after her parent's sent Pearl away, Papa grew
quiet and moody. He stopped tousling her hair
and calling her his little gem. She wondered if he
would ever get over Pearl's act of indiscretion
and the shame, she brought to the family being
with child out of wedlock.

One evening late in summer, a rap at the door
brought Papa to his feet. For the first time since Pearl
left, her father's face brightened. As he swung the door
open, he called out. "He's here."

Mama hurried into the front room; her eyes
twinkled. She brought her hands to her cheeks. "Robert,
so nice to see you again." She grabbed him by the arm
and pulled him inside. "Come in. Take a load off."

Edna studied the man with curiosity, even
though Mama warned her more than once about her

curiosity and how curiosity killed the cat. He was dressed all fancy, not in flannel shirts and heavy denim dungarees. Edna had only seen such formal attire on men at church or in town on Sundays when the townsfolk strolled the streets and men talked about work and women gossiped. Taller than her father, the stranger's presence loomed even larger with the height of his top hat.

"Edna, this is Mr. Barth, an old family friend. He's visiting all the way from Wisconsin. Can you say hello?"

Edna bobbed her head in greeting. "Hello, Mister Barth."

Mr. Barth squatted to Edna's eye level. He extended his hand. "Pleased to meet you, Edna. How are you this fine evening?"

Edna offered her hand and grinned, showing off her last missing tooth, as she grabbed Mr. Barth's hand. "I'm fine, thank you, Sir."

With a hearty chuckle straight from his belly, Mr. Barth straightened and tugged on his vest. "Good. Good."

Father led Mr. Barth into the front room. Mr. Barth handed his knee-length brown tweed overcoat and hat to Edna's mother and settled into the blue velvet settee. A shrill whistle from the teapot drew her mother's attention. She called to Edna and disappeared back into the kitchen. Mother placed several cookies on a porcelain plate. The whistle of the copper tea kettle faded. Mama poured herself a cup of hot water, then put it on a tray along with two cups of coffee and the cream and sugar bowls and headed to the living room.

Edna returned to their guest. "Would you care for a snickerdoodle?"

He smiled underneath his bushy red beard. Thanking her, he took two cookies and a napkin. He opened the cloth napkin across his lap as Edna's mother and lady friends did.

Mr. Barth took a bite then cocked his head. "Don't you have an older daughter? Pearl, isn't it? Is she here?"

Edna's jaw dropped. She stopped and stared at her father, waiting to see how he would explain her sister's absence.

Papa rubbed his chin before responding. "No, she's living in Seattle now, going to school, her final year."

Edna offered her father a cookie. After taking a single snickerdoodle, he set the plate on the table and nodded permission to Edna. She took a cookie and hurried to the Eastlake chair in the corner of the room, away from the adult conversation but still within hearing range.

Mr. Barth took a sip before speaking. "I'm glad you received my post. I'm here on business as I stated, but what a perfectly wonderful reason to visit old friends, eh, and see some of the sights of Seattle at the same time. How fortuitous that the Alaska Yukon Pacific Exhibition is going on during my stay."

Edna perked up. Some of her classmates boasted they would be going to Seattle during their summer break to see the sights of the first world's fair held in Seattle. Edna jumped off the chair and scooted it a bit closer to the conversation.

"Word is, this fair you're hosting is beyond anything offered at the World Fair in Philadelphia or even Portland, Oregon in 1905. The beauty of your mountain alone is worth the trip. It certainly surpasses any of the hills we have in Wisconsin."

Father took a gulp of what he called his daily boost. "It's a beautiful piece of the country here. Wait 'til you see the campus of the university, the site of the exposition. The main pavilion was built so visitors can see Mount Rainier from the grounds when they first enter." Father reached for a folded copy of the *Port Orchard Independent* on the coffee table. "Been keeping this here article since I received your post. The paper's got some great photographs of opening day." He tapped his index finger on the newspaper before handing it to his guest.

Mr. Barth skimmed it for a moment. "Says here, President Taft himself sent the signal that officially opened the Exposition, all the way from his desk at the White House."

Mama's face crumpled in confusion. "How is that possible?"

Mr. Barth read aloud. "The telegraph key was studded with gold nuggets taken from the first mine opened in the Klondike."

Straightening in his chair, Father nodded. "That's right, Abby. A single spark traveled across the lines all the way to Seattle. When the spark reached the Expo site, they struck a gong, unfurled a bunch of flags, and topped it all off with a twenty-one-gun salute. Yessiree, wish I'd been there. Bet that was a sight to see. Horns, whistles, and confetti, along with eighty-thousand people the first day alone. I imagine it left quite a mess for those street sweepers."

Though her cookie was long gone, Edna sat quietly, hanging on every word. Eyeing the plate of cookies, she craved another but didn't want to draw attention to herself since no one had shooed her from the room yet. Unable to hold back, she blurted out, "My friend, Inez, said they had fireworks."

136

Flashing a smile, Mr. Barth rubbed his chin. "My business associate from Washington visited last week. He told me it was the biggest fireworks show ever in the state, and dear friends, I'd be honored if the two of you and your daughter joined me as my guests at the fair."

No longer interested in cookies, Edna stared at Mr. Barth.

He cocked his head and flashed a grin in Edna's direction. "Would you like to go to the biggest fair this state has ever seen, young lady?"

Eyes as big around as the snickerdoodles, Edna looked from her mother to her father. "May we, Papa? Please."

Her father rubbed his beard like he did whenever he was considering something. "Sorry, Bob, I'm not a businessman like you. Got to return to work come Monday."

"Well, that settles it. We're all going to the world's fair tomorrow."

♪ ♪ ♪

She bounded out of bed early and rushed to the kitchen. Mr. Barth sat at the kitchen table with steam rising from his coffee cup. He looked up when she appeared. "Are you excited for the day?

Edna took a chair next to him and nodded furiously. "I sure am, Mr. Barth."

"My given name's Robert, but you can call me Uncle Buddy instead of Mr. Barth. Your parents are feeding the animals. As soon as they're done, we'll get going."

Two hours later, Uncle Buddy tossed a small train case along with a black leather bag onto the floorboard. He assisted Edna and her mother, then climbed up and took a seat up front next to Papa.

Spying the overnight bag, Edna raised her brows. "Are you leaving?"

"I'm here on business representing the Union Pacific Railroad. I'm glad to have enjoyed a night with your fine family, but after the fair tonight, the railroad is putting me up at the brand-new Hotel Sorrento while I conduct business."

Papa nodded. "I hear the Sorrento's a first-class place, supposed to have some amazing views of Elliott Bay."

The whip cracked, and Nellie whinnied and galloped away. July's heat had a hold on the day by eleven o'clock when the Athlon pulled into its slip at the Colman Dock. Scores of women and men dressed to the nines spilled down the gangplank.

Edna looked down at her pretty petticoat embroidered with blue flowers and her finest black, ankle-high shoes, and grinned. The crowd dashed toward the yellow trolleys that ran along the waterfront. With a firm grip on her mother's hand, Edna followed Uncle Buddy and Papa as they threaded their way through the crowd toward the street.

Her mother's grip tightened. "I've never seen such a crowd in my entire life. We don't want to become separated."

Papa put his arm around Mama's shoulders and guided her away from the scurrying throngs to the streetcar stand where trolleys with placards reading, *Alaska Yukon Exposition*, lined up in a long row. Onboard, Edna found a seat near the window. Mama picked up a copy of *The Seattle Times* someone left on

138

the seat and sat next to Edna. Uncle Buddy stood with a firm grip on a pole for support. With her nose against the glass, Edna took in every sight she passed: the huge brick stores of Frederick and Nelson and Wallin and Nordstrom. Though Inez and her mother sometimes shopped in the city, Mama never bought from these city stores. Sometimes, she ordered a pair of shoes or bloomers and corsets from the Sears and Roebuck catalog.

Mama read the paper, then turned to Uncle Buddy. "Says here half a million people visited the fair the first week alone."

"Wouldn't be surprised. It's made the news everywhere. It is, after all, called a world's fair."

In a matter of minutes, the trolley jerked to a stop. From the moment Edna stepped off the streetcar, she was mesmerized. Sunlight shone golden off the snow-capped peak of Mount Rainier, looming in the distance as if positioned there intentionally to impress the visitors from out of town. Men in dark suits or waistcoats and tall top hats or bowlers paraded with their best walking sticks. Heads held high. Women in their Sunday-best gowns, with their large, flowered bonnets with colorful feathers or sashes and long draped skirts or tailored dresses, strolled toward the University of Washington campus. Music soared above the crowd from yet unseen sights. The chattering of thousands of visitors melded like a gaggle of geese.

"We're here." Uncle Buddy swept his hand toward the most magnificent buildings Edna had ever seen. "What do you think?"

"Gracious." Mama held her hand over her open mouth. "I never could have imagined such a spectacle."

Following the pathway and the direction of the fairgoers, Edna walked between her new friend, Uncle Buddy, and her mother. The line for admission stretched over a block, but it pushed forward quickly. Father reached for his wallet, but Uncle Buddy waved off the offer. He pulled out two one-dollar bills for the three adult tickets and one child's fare. The ticket seller handed him a quarter in change. Uncle Buddy handed it to Edna with a wink.

Following the surge of people moving toward the main entrance, Papa pointed out the enormous silk rectangles attached to tall poles and waving in the wind. "These flags represent the many countries who have exhibits here."

"Wow." Edna tipped her head to see flags in colors more plentiful than those in her box of crayons. She didn't know which countries they represented, and she couldn't imagine counting them all.

Uncle Buddy handed their tickets to the uniformed ticket takers, and they were inside. Edna stared unblinking and wide-eyed at the sight of an enormous circular basin with a sign that read, *Geyser Basin*. In the middle, a fountain shot water high into the sky before splashing into the pool below. Arched buildings flanked each side. Uncle Buddy swept his arm across the courtyard and surrounding structures. "This called the Arctic Circle and the Cascade Waterfall."

"What's that?" Edna's eyes widened at the sight of the waterfall that appeared to spill out from at the entrance to an enormous, white-domed building.

"That's the Alaska Monument and the U.S. Government building, the largest building on the grounds. When it gets dark, they will light up each of the six waterfalls with different colored lights. It should be quite a sight."

Edna's father studied his old friend. "How do you know so much about our fair?"

Uncle Buddy reached into his jacket pocket and pulled out a crumpled booklet. "Some of my business associates visited last month. They told me all about it and gave me this guidebook." Buddy strode with quick steps toward the Alaska Building. Edna scurried past hundreds of people seated around the fountain. The wind caught spray off the fountain, tickling her face with a mist. She spun in a circle to take in the sheer size and wonder of it all. In the distance, behind the building-lined boulevards, lay a lush green lawn as far-stretching as the meadow behind her house.

"It's so beautiful." Edna gazed in awe at the tens of thousands of flowers, which bordered the blanket of green in neat fragrant plantings in a kaleidoscope of color.

Edna continued her hold on Mama's hand and quickened her steps to keep pace with the long-legged Uncle Buddy. Inside, Alaskan native artifacts filled the building.

Mama stopped in front of an exhibit, *Gold Camps of Alaska*. "Remember what I told you about your grandfather's gold claim?"

Edna recalled the letters her mother read to her. She'd even seen a few small nuggets Grandfather Mooney found when he went north. Now everywhere Edna looked, her eyes fell upon gold. Gold bricks, gold nuggets, gold jewelry. Beyond all the gold stood an igloo and two dogs. Edna pulled free from her mother and ran to the huskies.

Two Eskimos from Alaska, wearing buttonless shirts of animal hide and boots of fur, grinned, exposing their short teeth. "These dogs are part of a dog-sledding team."

A man hawking souvenirs called out. Edna turned to see him holding out a small doll. She ran to the souvenir stand. The man stroked the doll's fur coat and showed Edna the white fur boots. The doll was so different from her other dolls at home.

"What about you, little lady? Would you like an Eskimo doll?

"May I? Please?" She turned to Mama and pleaded.

Mother shook her head.

Edna held out her quarter. "But I have money."

Despite Mama's resistance, Uncle Buddy stepped forward with a few coins. "Please, let me. Your little girl should have a souvenir to remember this day."

The California exhibit looked and smelled like a giant produce market with tables spread with fruits and nuts. Edna turned a corner and stopped in her tracks. A life-size elephant stood on a large wooden base.

Uncle Buddy chuckled. "See that? The entire elephant is made from walnuts."

Further along, stood a full-size cow made from almonds and a bear made from raisins. Though her feet were tired, Edna trudged along, certain she would never see such amazing sights as these again in her life. It seemed the sights and sounds of the entire world stretched before her.

Beating drums up ahead drew Edna's attention. She tugged at her mother's coat. She slipped past a fellow with a funny flat hat pulling a small two-wheeled cart with two people aboard. Edna squeezed among the adults blocking the exhibit and stood on tiptoes to peek over the bamboo fencing that separated the display from the onlookers. Underneath a hut with a straw roof, she stared at a group of dark-skinned stubby men naked except for loincloths, like pictures she'd seen of American Indians. They had darker skin than the Indians and wore small hats resembling baskets atop

142

their short black hair. Zigzagged lines ran across their chests and covered their arms. Edna stood with her eyes wide and her mouth open as she watched the men chant in low guttural sounds stomping their feet and dancing with animated jerky movements while they beat on tom-tom drums made from animal skins. Mesmerized, Edna danced along with them. Beside them, another group of women and men crouched around a campfire. Edna blushed at the sight of the women, naked from the waist up, who poked at the embers with sticks, their eyes distant, emotionless. Mother found her way through the crowd and reclaimed Edna's hand with a sharp warning to stay close.

"Look, Mama. Who are they?"

"The sign says they're Igorrotes."

Behind the fence, straw and mud structures dotted the grounds. Edna edged closer to the sign that beckoned visitors to see for themselves the primitive wild people. "They're wearing hardly any clothes." Edna giggled.

Her mother glared and explained about the strange culture. "This is a savage tribe from the Philippines. They still eat dogs and people."

Her father's firm hand gripped her shoulder and prompted her away. "That's just a sensationalized exhibit intended to shock you. There are more suitable things to see."

Strolling past exhibits on agriculture and machinery, Papa fixed his gaze on an enormous log in the forestry building. "It's built from unhewed timber logs." He motioned Edna closer. "Look at this." He stood with his arms crossed as he read about the prized exhibit. "One-thousand-year-old log, sixteen feet in diameter. Even I've never seen anything this massive in all my years of bucking and loading logs."

At the familiar fluty sound of calliope music, Edna looked around. Spying the revolving horses in the distance, she tugged on her mother's sweater. "May I, please, Mama?" Edna pointed toward the carousel and held up her quarter. "I have money."

Papa nodded his approval, and Edna skipped the whole way to the amusement rides along a brick walkway wearing splotches of melted ice cream, spilled soda, and numerous fair confections. A sign marked the entrance to Pay Streak, and beyond that, lay a city block of exciting, inviting, magical rides and delicious and delightful, sumptuous treats. A fairy tale come true. Children waited in long queues for rides with amusing, thrilling names like 'Foolish House' and 'Tickler.' Buttery popcorn and spun sugary fluff of pink Fairy Floss rose above the heavy grease suspended in the air from burgers on the grill.

A call came from behind the concession stands. "Buy your raffle ticket. Only twenty-five cents."

Uncle Buddy motioned with his head in another direction. "Abby, you and Edna can check out the weekly raffle. Every week is something new, bushels of apples, baskets of nuts. Last week's prize was a milk cow. You never know what the prize is for the week. George and I are going to see the manned flying machine. We'll meet you at the carousel."

Edna and her mother headed off to see the raffle prize.

A gray-haired woman selling tickets smiled as she gripped a roll of tickets. "Get your tickets here, only two-bits. Win a beautiful, healthy baby boy."

Edna's eyes bulged. Surely, she'd heard wrong. Is this what Mama meant when she said Pearl had to give her baby away? Edna stared at her mother, who looked as shocked as Edna at the sight of the woman collecting coins from interested spectators and handing them red raffle tickets.

"The child is only one month old. Step forward and see for yourself what a handsome lad he is."

Unable to hide her shock, Edna tugged at her mother's sleeve. "Is this what is going to happen to Pearl's baby?"

Her mother's gaze jerked from Edna to the middle-aged woman in a white uniform and a white hat. "No. Of course not. Pearl's baby will be delivered in a facility with good standing and will be placed for adoption to a proper home."

Edna read the sandwich board advertising the raffle and bearing a poster of a chubby-cheeked baby. *Washington Children's Home Society.* "This place says it's a children's home. What if the place you give the baby to sells it? How do you know her baby won't be given away like a cow?"

"What?" Her mother studied the sign and the woman who was selling tickets for a chance to win a baby. "Come along. We need to go."

Edna looked over her shoulder as Mother led her away and toward the carousel. Her head whirled with unanswered questions.

After the sun went down, the air turned chilly. Amidst the dark, cloudless sky, lights came on from every corner of the fairground, illuminating the displays and inviting people to linger and to see more sights. Fireworks soared across the sky over Elliot Bay, fanning out in bursts of red, white, blue, and gold. All Edna could think about was the baby boy who was being raffled off. What would become of Pearl's baby? Would the innocent child be snatched away from Pearl and vanish as quickly as the flashes of light streaking through the sky?

ABOUT THE AUTHOR

Naomi Wark is a life-long resident of Washington. Upon retiring, Naomi moved to Camano Island and after finishing their home, focused on her long-ignored passion of writing. With the support from fellow writers with the Skagit Valley Writer's League, she published her debut novel, *Wildflowers in Winter* in 2017. The excerpt published here, Alaska Yukon Pacific Exposition is from her prequel novel, *Songs of Spring*, to be released soon. The entry is a third-place winner in the SVWL literary short story contest. Her other awards include two, second place awards with EPIC Group Writers. The theme of Naomi's books is family and how family relationships shape each of us. When she is not writing, Naomi enjoys gardening, volunteering for the Stanwood Camano Food Bank, and family, especially her grandchildren. Her book can be found at Seaport Books and on Amazon.

Visit Naomi's author Facebook page and her website:
http://naomiwarkauthor.com

Sully A Dobbs

QUICKSAND

There is none such thing as freedom,
No matter where you go,
No matter what you abandon,
No matter how you show,

A trail of chains will take their turns,
To rattle, clamp, and close,
You think you've got one unlocked now,
But oh look! Another's got your toes.

Escape the prison you've made yourself,
And now the rhythm's locked its doors,
Find the key to open the hatch,
But it's only you outside, looking back,

Maybe there's some kind of bliss,
Or compromise for in-between.
But no, there is nothing there,
No freedom to be seen.

Sully A Dobbs

BREAKING EGGSHELLS

I am a bird, and I cannot fly,
Whether or not the trees sway,
And their leaves touch the sky,
I remain still, and here I stay.

But don't you want to soar, and watch the passersby?

That would be lovely,
But I have no wings,
And I'd rather rest here,
Then listen to you sing.

But they sit right beside you, do they not?

Yes, I'm afraid,
But the feathers are clipped,
They are useless now,
Like the leap of your lip.

But why just sit here, why not chirp to pass the time?

Oh, I assure you,
My beak works just fine,

But I wouldn't chat,
For the price of your dime.

But how do you live, without wings to give you life?

To be perfectly clear,
I shall repeat by words instead,
And hopefully then,
They'll break through your head.

I am a bird, and I cannot fly,
Whether or not the trees sway,
And their leaves touch the sky,
I remain still, and here I stay.

For I am not broken,
You just don't like my ways.

ABOUT THE AUTHOR

At sixteen years old, Sully A. Dobbs is currently the youngest member of the Skagit Valley Writers league. She won third place in the poetry competition. She is an aspiring author. She likes writing stories in the genres of horror, and urban, and historical fantasy. She hopes that she will soon be able to make one of her stories into a novel.

Bruce Lawson

THE FRENCH DOLL

She had that funny way of tapping her foot and swaying her hips when she was deep in thought or upset and that's what she was doing this morning when I walked into the kitchen.

"Karen, sweetheart, what's wrong?"

"I didn't sleep much."

"I know, you tossed and turned all night."

"Sorry sweetie didn't mean to keep you awake."

"Are you expecting someone? You keep looking out the window?"

"Liana Davidson should drive in at any moment; she has a doll for me to dress. That's why I'm nervous."

"Don't let yourself get worked up dear, remember it's just a doll. Liana brings lots of her dolls for you to dress, what's so special about this one?"

Ignoring my question she asked, "Honey, would you get the sewing machine out of the closet and put the extra leaf in the dining room table for me?"

153

"Sure, if you tell me what's so remarkable about this doll?"

"I haven't seen it. Only thing Liana told me is that it's a 34-inch *Emile Jumeau* doll that belongs to the woman who owns the Great American Doll Company in Bellevue, and it's expensive."

"Who's this *Emile Jumeau*?"

"Just one of the top Parisian doll makers of the late eighteen hundred, is all."

"You said expensive, how expensive? Do we have to get a rider on our house insurance to cover it?"

"I don't know about the insurance, dear. My concern is if I can dress it right."

As I went to get the sewing machine I thought, this is the first time in our twenty-five years of marriage I'd heard my wife doubt herself when it came to her artistic talents. While I struggled to put the leaf on the table, Liana showed up, her usual carefully coiffured blond hair in disarray. She carried a long glass topped box. I knew it was obvious, but I asked anyway, "Is that the doll?"

"Yes, it's the doll Bruce; would you please move the sewing machine so I can put it down? I've had a busy morning; I'm beat and she's heavy."

Well, that was Liana, two minutes into the house and already giving orders. After doing her bidding, I joined the ladies who were examining the doll and said without thinking, "You know, with her eyes closed, she looks like she's in a coffin." As soon as the words left my mouth, I knew that was the wrong thing to say, and mumbled a quick, "Sorry, I was just trying to be funny." The two unsmiling faces turned away from me and looked at the doll.

Liana slid open the glass top. My wife gasped. "Oh, my God she's beautiful."

I was speechless, captivated by the life-like face. How, I wondered, did those French doll makers learn to fire

154

bisque porcelain in such a way as to get that skin-like finish? "The body's leather," I said, touching it.

"It's more than that," Liana said, reaching under the doll. "It's an original *Chevrot* hinged body with excellent porcelain legs and those lovely bisque arms and perfect hands and fingers. You're right it is leather but it's bleached kid goat leather and in excellent condition for its age. Do you see there are no patches, the seams are tight and it's still firm and well rounded? Amazing, for being well over a hundred years old. It's in such fine shape I don't think children played with it."

I tried to be funny again, "If you attached strings, it could be a puppet."

Karen wasn't amused. I'm not going to describe the look she gave me, but rest assured it wasn't pleasant. Jabbing me in the ribs, she asked, "Do you have anything else of importance to add, dear?"

"No, but I get your point. I think I'll just stand here, quiet like, and watch."

"That would be nice," she said, helping Liana lift the doll from the box.

Placed on its stand, the doll's eyes slowly opened and for a moment, with the way her head tilted, I thought she too scolded me for thinking she was a puppet. I looked closer at the dark glass eyes; drawn in by the life-like look in the black pupils and brown irises. They were so real, so alive, I had to turn away and remind myself it was only a doll.

Liana watched my reaction and smiled. "It's unreal isn't it, the way those doll makers, those artists; made their creations so life-like? You and Karen have been to the Louvre in Paris and seen Michelangelo's wonderful sculptures. Seeing what he did with a block of marble and what this doll maker did with a handful of clay, you understand what I mean." Liana walked around the table and studied the doll from all angles. "It's the little things, the details, the finely painted eyebrows and lashes, the hint of eye shadow, a touch of blush on the cheeks and the pierced ears. Look at her lips, though closed, that slight upturn on the right corner of her

155

mouth gives her a captivating look, doesn't it? And who knows? These artists lived in Paris where the Mona Lisa is hung. Maybe that was this doll maker's inspiration." Silent, I took in the beauty Liana pointed out.

"See the shape of her face, the hint of chin and the beautiful brunette human hair wig, with its long banana curls, it all comes together and gives her personality. As you both know, I make my own brand of dolls, but the glass eyes I buy are nothing compared to these. Look closely, they draw you into their depths. I wish I could make a doll of this quality, one with this much character, one that makes you think she's speaking to you, to you alone."

Liana's enthusiasm caught hold of me, and I whispered, "*Mon Cherie*, forgive me for calling you a puppet."

Later that week coming home from my railroad job, I found Karen amongst boxes of antique cloth and lace, threading a needle.

"How's it going?"

"Take a look for yourself. I'm almost finished with the *culottes*."

"*Culottes*?"

"That's French for panties, honey."

The doll's face was turned down and away, so I couldn't see the eyes but with the way she was scantily dressed and the blush on her cheek, she gave the impression of modesty and embarrassment.

"I've just a few more stitches to make and I'll have the lace trim finished, then I can make a slip for her."

"I'm sure she'd appreciate that, sweetheart. Say, is it warm enough here?"

"It's comfortable to me dear. Why do you ask?"

"You're going to laugh, but I have no clue why I asked that."

156

"I know why you did, Sweetheart. Even though you'll think what I'm going to say is silly, you're concerned for the doll's comfort, just as you would be if it were a real child."

"That's weird; I didn't realize I was doing that."

"Honey, the doll's so real looking it's easy to do. Our minds play tricks on us. For example, if we see the head turned a certain way or shoulders slumped, we transfer that to a human action. Dolls are made in our likeness, especially these French ones. We're easily taken in. I poked her with a needle and caught myself saying, "Sorry.""

As the days slipped by, I saw my wife's confidence change from unsure to in charge, as the dressing progressed. She'd finished off the *culottes* with delicate pale pink and lavender ribbon and the slip and thigh high stockings with lace.

She said with a smile, as she turned the doll around, "This completes the under garments, now I can get on with her dress." I set a cup of tea next to the sewing machine and asked,

I set a cup of tea next to the sewing machine. "Have you figured out what you're going to do?"

"Liana told me the doll's original 1880's clothing has been packed away and the owner wanted her doll dressed in the fashions of 1910."

"The flapper era?"

"No, that wasn't until the twenties. By 1910 the stiff Victorian era of full skirts, bustles and high collars had ended. Women's dresses now were made of light cotton or linen, gathered at the waist by belt or sash. They were scandalous for the times with open necklines. Styles flowed loosely to just above the ankles and were festooned with colorful ribbons. They were quite gay and appropriate for parties and casual outdoor wear. That's the kind of dress I plan to make."

"Is that what the woman who owns the doll wants?"

"My instructions were for a 1910 style. That's all. What I come up with is of my choosing: my design, my choice of materials. When I'm done, it will be what she wants, but it will be my creation."

"You're pretty emphatic about that, aren't you?"

"Honey, I was hired to dress a doll, that's a lot different from being a tailor sewing together someone else's idea. Could you imagine the artist who sculpted this doll's head putting up with someone standing behind him saying, "I think you should pinch the nose a little more?"

"I see your point."

"Thanks, now I better get on with it."

The doll, at least for me, felt like one of the family. While cooking dinner one evening, I felt the doll watching me. It didn't matter where I was in the room or which way she was turned; she was always looking at me. It could be out of the corner of her eye, straight ahead or nonchalant from the side. The same was true of the mouth; the side with the slight smile gave her a mischievous look, the side with the straight lips, questioning. I could see how children up and talk to their dolls.

Karen finished the flowing summer dress, keeping the lavender trim simple, so as not to detract from the doll's lovely face. The last piece of the doll's wardrobe was a light pale grey jacket, of lamb's wool. Karen asked where she could get some ermine to trim the collar and I suggested a taxidermy shop and told her I'd look one up in the yellow pages.

My third call was a gold mine. She, yes it was a women taxidermist, was not only able to get an ermine pelt, but managed to find a piece of kid-goat leather that Karen made into stylish, 1910 ankle high button shoes.

So, two months from start to finish, the doll stood complete. The finishing touches included amber earrings and a beaded purse that hung from a strap off her shoulder. "She looks great, dear," I said. "She looks proud. Remember how apprehensive you were at the start and look at the doll now."

My wife smiled with satisfaction as she snapped shut the lid on her sewing machine. Next evening, I came home from work, anticipating seeing the doll, but the dining room table was bare. The sewing machine is gone. The boxes of antique cloth are gone. The doll is gone. Only a linen runner and a bowl of pink and white petunias were on the table. I fantasized the house was broken into and the doll stolen and held in some dangerous place for ransom. Or she really was a puppet and had thrown off the trapping so lovingly put on her, and like Pinocchio, ran off with a traveling circus. But those fanciful thoughts dimmed as a touch of loneliness crept in, bringing the same empty feelings as when the kids left home. Karen came in munching on a celery stick and saw me slumped in the easy chair. "Why the long face?"

"I didn't expect she'd be gone so soon."

"Honey, I know you're bummed, but Liana came by this afternoon unexpectedly, picked up the doll and paid me off. So, to both of our regrets, our beautiful little house guest is gone. But enough of that, I've got dinner almost ready so why don't you get out of those work clothes and jump in the bath. And while you're in there put a smile on your face and remember your words when Liana first brought her here. Do you remember what you said to me that day?"

I looked up and nodded. "Yeh, I said it's just a doll."

Bruce Lawson

BUCHAREST

It is 1970, we're sixty miles south of Bucharest, Romania, and the cold war's been a stalemate for twenty years. Word has come through crypto channels the Russians have developed a secret weapon, one that will upset the balance of power. Worried, England and the United States have dispatched their top agents. CIA's Donald Woodman and his British counterpart, M2's Reginald Heatherton, behind the iron curtain in disguise to steal the secrets.

***

"I dare say Donald, old chap, it's top rate to be working with you again, but I have to ask did you have a choice in your disguise for this assignment."

"Yes, I did Reginald, and I see you picked the same one I did."

"Oh no, old boy, this one is a favorite of mine. I've used this German dog disguise many times. Why just last spring when I foiled the Chinese spy, Cho Chi Chung, in Singapore, I used it."

160

"I read about that caper my friend, but weren't you wearing a Pekinese dog outfit that time?"

"I say, old bean, you caught me there, jolly good of you to jog the old memory. I did wear that cute Pekinese disguise. Loved that rhinestone collar that came with it but had the devil of a time with those Chinese dogs sniffing about."

"Reginald, you know I'm not fond of riding in car trunks, but you have to admit we haven't had any trouble with the border guards as yet."

"I'd say we've pulled a bit of wool over their eyes, old boy. Our Russian driver thinks we're gifts for Nikita Khrushchev. Won't he be surprised when we toddle off to track down Field Marshal Bigoffski, and pull the same scheme on him we used last year on that devious Spanish dwarf, El Greco Fredo, and steal the plans."

"The El Greco Fredo double switch, capital idea Reginald."

"Donald, would you be so kind as to do me a favor? I'm not able to scratch my left ear,

could you do it for me? I'd give a shilling to know which one of the chaps wore this outfit last. It seems to be full of those little creatures."

"What, fleas?"

"I dare say yes, old boy."

"I'm afraid you're out of luck there pal, I'm in the same boat as you when it comes to scratching."

"Boat, that's a quaint term to use old man, seeing we're riding in the trunk of a car, speaking of which have you noticed anything different about this car, ole bean?"

"It's a 58 Plymouth, why?"

"You old tot. I know it's a 58 Plymouth, but why does it have holes for our heads to stick out? M2 would never spend money on something like this. No, I have a suspicion this might be…"

"What Reginald?"

"A bloody trap!"

"You think! Maybe we should escape while we have the chance?"

"Capital idea, let me get the trunk keys."

"Reginald, I don't like the look on your face, what's wrong?"

"The keys, old boy, I left them on the hotel nightstand."

"You left them? How could you do that?"

"No pockets old chap."

"I suppose that means you don't have a crowbar either?"

***

Meanwhile twenty miles north in a chateau nestled in the Mountains on Romania's northern border Russian master spy, Natasha Vondoloski, up to her pretty neck in a bubble bath, is on the phone.

"I know Boris darling, their car crossed the border last night, there's nothing to worry about, I have it under control. The fools disguised themselves as German shorthair dogs, supposedly a gift for Nikita." "What's that? Speak louder Boris there is something wrong with your phone. I can hardly understand you. What was that you asked?"

"Boris, I said they came across the border disguised as German short hair dogs. I repeat German short hairs."

"Boris, not Germans with short hair. I didn't say that."

"Now you're jumping to conclusions, Boris."

"I most emphatically did not say German soldiers crossed the border."

"Boris, I will not hang up so you can warn the Kremlin."

"For crying out loud Boris the war with Germany ended twenty-five years ago."

"Boris"

"Damn, he hung up."

***

Plymouth lurched off the pavement onto the gravel road leading to Natasha's chateau. Our spies huddled in the trunk.

"Didn't I tell you to not drink that last cup of tea this morning Reginald? Remember my warning; if you drink that cup, you'll want to stop every five minutes, didn't I say that? Now look at you, every time the car hits a bump you let out a moan and expect sympathy from me. Well, you're not going to get it this time, do you hear? You are British, before you do anything you have to have your cup of tea; well, you can just lay there and suffer for all I care."

"You've been warned before; remember the diamond heist in Durban South Africa we foiled? We had the Mongolian assassin Malign Khan, trapped in the mine shaft and what did you do just when we closed in for the capture? Don't lay there and give me that I don't remember look you know perfectly well what you did. In fact, I tell you what you did, you walked away, yes you walked away and why did you walk away. Do you remember why you walked away? Do you want me to remind you why you walked away? Well, if you're just going to lay there and look dumb thinking, I'll just let this go, then you have another thought coming. I remember those five words. Not five words I made up to make you look bad, but your exact words. I can still hear those words as if you spoke to them two minutes ago. They are as clear as a bell to me. Clear as the bell that calls me to church in Schenectady. Not loud and brassy kike your New Westminster bell that hurts one's ears when it rings."

"Something else mister, I'm going to have another cup of tea, you did the same thing when we were in that rat infested slum in Sao Paulo, Brazil. I tried to get you to help me stabilize the building before the roof caved in and brought the orphanage full of children sliding down the hillside into the

163

chemical plant. Do you remember that and what the Queen said to you when you finally got the nerve to go back home, do you?"

"I could go on and on. How about the time we stole the Russian submarine disguised as Eskimo diamond smugglers or when we freed the cruise ship, *Happy Vacations*, from the Madagascar hijackers, and you in what I consider your best disguise to date. A blind Hindu beggar on a cruise ship was brilliant but I thought you carried it a bit far when you kept stumbling around bumping into things, spilling your drinks and then falling off the ship. Well mister, another cup of tea, that ship's captain wasn't going to stop and rescue you until I revealed who you really were. And as I remember you never did thank me for that, ...but that's okay. That's just the way you brits are..."

"On all those capers you said the same five words and I thought for the longest time you had them written down so you would always say them the same way, but now I believe you have learned them in school. Think me a crazy conspiracy nut if you like, but I think all Brits are taught the same thing. In fact, I can picture you right now at the black board writing those five words."

"I'm not going to try and guess at what age you're taught this standard British line, no doubt decreed by the Queen"

"I should clarify that. I have no firsthand knowledge of what the Queen might have decreed, so do not hold me to it. But if I were asked by someone who really wanted to know what age you were, I'd say eight years old. That is when American kids are learning to write sentences, but do not think for one minute that American kids are going to write something the Queen decrees, no not in your life. We had a revolution to get rid of all that Queen decree's nonsense a long time ago."

"Oh, now look at you yawn, acting like this is boring, well I'm not finished yet. I can still see you at the blackboard, a skinny eight-year-old, short pants, and knobby knees. Oh yah, now you say you were six and already knew how to write a full sentence and was in long pants. What are you trying to do make American kids look stupid? That's something I won't

164

put up with, mister another cup of tea. I'll defend our kids to the bitter end."

"What's that? Now you are trying to change the subject. You are embarrassed by what the Queen has taught you, am I right? Be brave Reginald, I'm not going to broadcast it to the world."

"Donald, old chap, the cars stopped so shut up. I've got to go potty."

"See Reginald, there are those five words again."

***

Meanwhile, outside the car, in front of her Chateau, Natasha talks with the driver.

"Malkavich, stay in the car we have to leave right away."

"Why?"

"Boris darling has told the Kremlin; Germans have crossed the border."

"I didn't hear that on the radio."

"You won't, it's a figment of Boris's imagination."

"So, there's nothing to worry about then?"

"I didn't say that. We might have the whole Russian army coming here any minute, that's why we have to leave now!"

***

"Reginald, did you hear that, she said the whole Russian army?"

"I wasn't listening, old bean, I'm trying to get the trunk open; I've got to go potty bad"

"Like I've said a million times Reginald, you Brits drink far too much tea."

"Don't go there again old chap."

"Listen, I'd know that voice anywhere, that's Kristina Koskavich outside the car?"

"You're wrong, old boy, doesn't sound like her at all?"

"If not her, who…?"

"Natasha?"

"Natasha, has more nasal in her voice."

"Had Donald. Remember I'm the M2 agent who parachuted into Stalingrad, disguised as the eminent doctor, Vidamar Pulaski, and implanted the GPS in her."

"What's that got to do with her nasal tones if I might ask"

"Well old tot at the time I did the implant I gave her a nose bob."

"A nose bob? I thought she looked different when I bumped into her in the Paris catacombs."

"I know it was cheeky of me to do it but as you well know I've always liked to tidy things up a bit. Speaking of which, I do have to go potty, and it looks like they're not going to open the trunk."

"What can we do Reginald?"

"Bark."

"What?"

"Bark like a dog, we're disguised as them, old chap."

"Woof."

"What?"

"Woof."

"That's not a bark, Donald."

"Yes, it is, Reginald."

"A woof is not a bark, ole man."

166

"Yes, it is"

"No, it's not and I can prove it."

"How?"

"Easy, let us say I'm a burglar and you had a dog that barked. I would run away."

"You would?"

"Yes, but if your dog woofed that wouldn't scare me, and I would rob you."

"Really?"

"Yes."

"I guess I don't really know you."

"What do you mean by that, ole chap?"

"Now I've got to count the silverware every time you come to visit."

"What the devil are you talking about ole bean?"

"You, being a burglar and all."

"Where did you get that hair-brained Idea?"

"From you."

"What?"

"Just now you said you wouldn't be scared of my dog if he woofed and you would rob me, isn't that, right?"

"Donald, seeing we're locked in the trunk of this car and chances of carrying out our assignment is looking bleak, indulge yourself, old boy and woof if you want."

To be continued.

ABOUT THE AUTHOR

Writer Bruce Lawson is fortunate to have been born in the Puget Sound area and raised in the unique surroundings of the Northwest. When three of his five grandchildren moved to Virginia, he would write simple short stories weekly for their mother to read to them at bedtime. One of these stories, The Grey Rabbit with Black Ears is published in the Anthology *Tales for a Lazy Afternoon*. Other short stories became chilling adventure, tales of bear encounters in the wilds of Alaska, Wyoming, and Montana. A coming-of-age novel is in the works. This year Bruce received a Literary Award from Skagit Valley Writers League for his nonfiction story *The French Doll* and he received an Honorable Mention from Write on the Sound for his short story *The Car Salesman's Bear* in 2017.

Kathleen Kaska

ACROPHOBIA

I step out of the car and lean
toward the ground. The incline
Invisible to my eyes but ever
so present in my brain.
I grab ahold of the street sign on
Angle Street to keep from sliding
down the mountain and off
the face of the earth—
a drop-off somewhere
at the bottom of the valley
across the road boldly
named the Sea to Sky Highway.

In the restaurant, my soup tilts
in my bowl and cherry tomatoes roll
to the side of my salad plate,
caught by the sliced cucumbers
secure in their flatness.
The gravity tugs my cheek
and I look as if I have a form of palsy.

Not until we cross the river
onto level ground
does the feeling of vertigo
leave my head and pull down
another victim driving from
sea level up to the crest of
the Cascade Mountains.

Kathleen Kaska

MOVING MOON

In the dark morning, I wake,
surprised to find a waxing moon perched
in the upper pane of my bedroom window,
setting there like a Warhol painting.

Half-moon in East Window.
Soon the white sickle will slide from view,
leaving behind a yellow haze.
a reminder that it will return
the same time next year

.
But will I be awake to notice
if it has changed, a wrinkle
marring its smooth surface?

Before it disappears, I reach out
and hang my hopes on its hook—
a dangling bag of wishes
carried around the globe
on the tail of a celestial kite.

ABOUT THE AUTHOR

Kathleen Kaska is the author of *The Sherlock Holmes Quiz Book*, published by Rowman & Littlefield Publishing Group in 2020. She founded The Dogs in the Nighttime, the Sherlock Holmes Society of Anacortes, Washington, a scion of The Baker Street Irregulars.

Kathleen also writes three awarding-winning mystery series: the Sydney Lockhart Mystery Series, the Kate Caraway Animal-Rights Mystery Series, and the Classic Triviography Mystery Series. Her book, *Do You Have a Catharsis Handy? Five Minute-Writing Tips* won first-place in the Chanticleer International Book Award in the non-fiction Instruction and Insights category. Her poem, "Moving Moon," received Honorable Mention in Skagit Valley Writers League 2021 Literary Awards for Poetry.

Kathleen teaching writing and coaches' new writers. The name of her business is Metaphor Writing Coach. Sign up for her newsletter and read her blog post, "Growing Up Catholic in a Small Texas Town."

Contact Kathleen at:

http://www.kathleenkaska.com

https://metaphorwritingcoach.com/

kathleenkaska@hotmail.com

Kim E. Kimmy

"THE "CAPUHTILLAR"

I spied him as he entered the fast-food restaurant with his mother, and surmised he was about four years old. The cute little guy was inquisitive about everything as small boys often are, and his asking why and what about each thing he observed from his below-the-counter vantage point amused me.

As my husband and I munched our meals, making quiet conversation, the little boy finished his, and surprisingly made a beeline to my side across the restaurant. Although I was a stranger, he was anxious to show me the toy from his child's meal. I glanced at his mother to make sure she was comfortable with this, and she smiled, nodding that he had her permission.

In one hand was an action figure, and in the other was a green, plastic, movable wormlike toy caterpillar. As he babbled about his action figure, I asked what was in his other hand, "Oh, that's my capuhtillar," he nonchalantly explained. Pronouncing it correctly, I asked if he knew what happened to caterpillars when they grow up. This preschooler did not

173

know. With my best low magical-like voice I revealed, "They turn into butterflies." Wide-eyed, he nearly shouted, "They do not!"

As his mother was approaching our table, I reiterated within her earshot, "Yes, they really do turn into butterflies when they grow up. Ask your mom." He kept his eyes on me as his mother quietly affirmed, "The nice lady is right. They do."

In an exasperated voice, he again vehemently argued, "They do not! They are fuzzy and they live in the dirt and caputillars do *not* turn into butterflies." Seeing an opportunity for a life lesson, I quietly described the process of metamorphosis, and how it is critically important not to help the caterpillar out of the cocoon. I expounded on how we sometimes have to do tasks and chores that are hard and we want help, but if we do them ourselves it makes us stronger, just as the butterfly's new wings become by struggling its way out of a cocoon.

My new little friend listened intently, pondered my story, finally shaking his head, and loudly and somewhat disgustedly concluded with his announcement, "Caputillars do *not* turn into butterflies." He gave me an accusing look, as though I were a mean person telling lies to a vulnerable child. I suggested maybe his mom could show him in a book, and she nodded, suggesting her generation's preferred research method of looking on the computer.

He eyed me somewhat warily as I bade him goodbye, and he walked out holding his mother's hand, yet keeping me within his sight until they exited the restaurant. Soon my husband and I went to our car. It was sunny and I decided it was a convertible day. My car is a model with a hinged hardtop. Its clever engineering folds into the trunk in about twenty seconds. As I was about to push the button, I spotted my little friend in the car beside us as his mom was strapping him into his car seat while he studied his plastic caterpillar that he'd been told has even more fantastic and realistic ability than the action figure in his other hand. He spotted me too and squinted a wary eye at me. With a grin, I couldn't resist asking him if he wanted to see something almost as magical as a caterpillar turning into a butterfly. He actually sighed, rolled his eyes and reluctantly resigned to answer affirmatively, muttering, "Okay, I guess."

I pushed the button, which releases the roof causing it to fold as the trunk opens allowing the metal roof and glass rear windshield to nest into it in a manner of seconds.

Eyes wider than when he heard the caterpillar revelation, he gaped open- mouthed. I thought he was rendered speechless until he nearly shouted as I waved goodbye backing out, "I'm telling my dad about you!"

ABOUT THE AUTHOR

Kim E. Kimmy of Anacortes is a non-fiction humor writer who specializes in seeing the humor of everyday occurrences. She has also written a children's book entitled "Locked Out in the Snow," and a keepsake memory book meant for gift giving entitled "Special Occasion Memories." She is an emcee and speaker who enjoys entertaining groups.

Donna M. Rudiger

SKAGIT BEAUTY

The sunshine enticed me out to play this morning.
Mother Nature is showing off, she wants to be admired and
photographed.
With adventurer's anticipation
I pack cameras, notebooks, sunscreen, and drive north to the
flats.
Skagit Beauty is modeling centerfolds of color across the
topography,
blankets of tulips carpet the fields in bands of red, yellow, and
magenta,
their petals lifted heavenward, reaching for the sun's rays.
The aroma of freshly spread manure clears the alder pollen
from my sinuses.
A tractor hums alongside the road, turning last season's
fallow ground,
releasing the organic perfumes of the chocolate-colored
earth.
Red-tailed hawks circle above, watching, waiting for signs of
rodent life.
In the background, the sun-lit radiance of Mount Baker
fills the noon sky with penetrating luminescence.
And all the people come...in cars, by bus, on foot and
bicycles.
Observers of earth's glory marching through mud and tall
grasses,
seeking a divine encounter with
the sacred ceremonies of spring in the Pacific Northwest!

Donna M. Rudiger

NEW VOICES OF QUIET DESPERATION

Today, I heard the roar of silence
beckoning from the other side of my denial.
Previously muted by overwhelm and uncertainty,
my poetic voice screams for artistic release.
Using familiar acclamations, I extend edification to my
tribe.
Discouraged souls who no longer embrace or trust
empty rhetoric and false bravados, their
hearts wait in despair for changes that will not manifest.
The blessed voices of creation are vanquished,
threatened by differences both imagined and real,
ignited by misunderstanding and fear.
Rebuking the patronizations of the elite,
my pen becomes my weapon,
a freshly sharpened sword.
Liquid light inks every page,
Holy breath blankets the words, and
publishes truth, healing, and restorative energy.
A new alliance has begun.
Now, I look directly into the eyes of everyone I meet.
Observing my reflection in the mirrors of their soul,
I extend a glance of peace and acceptance.
Allowing the compassion submerged in me to surface
as a smile,
I discover, without judgment, their humanity and spirit.
I chose to be the illumination they need for one dark
moment in their day.
I share the riches of kindness and empathy, piercing
their
brokenness with the presence of spiritual vitality.
I speak hope with a jubilant voice and dissolve their
present darkness.
Our uncertainty holds unlimited possibility!

ABOUT THE AUTHOR

Donna started writing poetry at age 13 while she was growing up in Pennsylvania. Her love of the Cascade Mountains inspired her to migrate to the Pacific Northwest in 1974 to study wildlife photography. She is an award-winning poet, essayist, and storyteller, and cheerfully shares her work at women's retreats as well as numerous open-mike venues in Western Washington. Her poem titled "Skagit Beauty" was first published in *Soundings from the Salish Sea* in 2018 (available on Amazon.com) And then featured in the Edmonds News Poetry Corner in March 2020. Her poem titled "New Voices for Quiet Desperation" was recently published in the Edmonds News Poetry Corner in March 2021.

Donna can be reached at donna.beamer66@gmail.com or on Facebook at https://www.facebook.com/donna.rudiger.

Clark Graham

A PAST LIFE

The weight of his briefcase felt strangely unfamiliar. He gazed down at it. *Is it even mine?*

A limousine pulled up to the curb. The driver, in a blue uniform and a chauffer's hat, jumped out and opened the door for him. "Mr. Percy, how are you doing today? It's a good thing your meeting let out early. We can beat rush hour traffic if we leave now."

"Who are you?"

"Oh, I'm sorry. My name is Charles. Your normal driver is ill today. I'll be driving you home."

Looking up and down the street, Mr. Percy finally asked. "Are you sure you're picking up the right person?"

"Yes, Marty sent me your picture. See, here it is." The driver held up his phone for Mr. Percy to see. "Rough day, huh?"

He shook his head. He couldn't contradict the man. His memory of anything was a blur. "I guess. Take me home please, Charles."

"Right away, Sir."

Mr. Percy sat down in the nice soft seat and stretched out. Scanning the limo, he shook his head again. *I have no memory of this. It has to be a dream.* He leaned back and closed his eyes. *It will end when I wake up, but meanwhile, I'm enjoying it.*

An hour later, the limo pulled up to a huge three-story house with an ivy-covered stone front. Charles came around and opened the door for him. "There you go, Sir. Welcome home."

Mr. Percy stood in front of the house, looking up. "Are you sure of the address?" He already knew what Charles would say but had to ask it anyway.

"Yes, this is the one Marty texted me. Go on in and see if they recognize you. I'll stay here a minute in case you need to go somewhere else."

Mr. Percy walked up to the door, swung open before he could extend his hand. A butler in tails bowed. "Mr. Percy, welcome home. Come and sit and I'll grab your favorite snack while you wait for the cook to finish your dinner."

He pinched himself, but it didn't wake him. He followed the butler in. A large two-story entryway with a chandelier hanging down greeted him. The butler led him into a study lined with old-looking books. The butler led him to an overstuffed leather chair with a lamp behind it. A bowl of peanuts mixed with chocolate chips sat on the end table next to the chair. When he sat down the butler disappeared down the hall, but quickly came back with a glass of cold water. "The cook says dinner will be served in a few minutes."

He snacked on some of the peanuts and chocolate. *I do remember liking this. I wonder where from?*

A younger woman in an apron came into the library. "Sir, your dinner is served."

"I'm having problems with my memory. What's your name?"

"Camella, Sir."

"What's my first name?"

She giggled. "Morgan, but we're not allowed to call you that."

"How long have you worked for me, Camella?"

"Um, four years now."

Morgan stood up from the chair. "Lead the way." *She doesn't look a day over sixteen. Did I hire her at twelve?*

They made their way into the dining room. He sat down in front of the only place setting at the end of a long oak table. The cook, a large woman in a white chef's hat and apron set a stuffed pork loin with carrots and a small salad in front of him. "Bon Appetit," she said.

Camella poured him a glass of red wine.

"Oh, I don't drink."

"Sorry," she took the wine away.

I don't drink. How do I know that and don't remember anything else? Why didn't she know I didn't drink? She should have said something either way.

He scanned the empty room. He sat alone. All the servants had retreated. Chewing the pork chop slowly, he savored it before he swallowed. He didn't care much for the carrots, but the salad he ate.

As if on cue, the girl came back and took his plate as soon as he finished. "Didn't like your carrots?" she asked.

"No."

"I'll make a note for the cook not to serve you those anymore."

"Thanks." Nothing seemed right. This couldn't be his home. Why didn't the servants know his likes and dislikes?

The butler came in. "Do you wish to watch television this evening, Sir, or shall I bring you a newspaper?"

"What's on tonight, that I like?" He toyed with the man.

"Frankly, Sir, I hand you the remote and you watch what you will."

He got me there. "I'll just take the newspaper." He headed back into the library where he found a copy of the paper on his overstuffed chair. When bedtime came, he wanted to wander around the house and check it out, but the assistant cook was waiting outside the library.

"I'll show you to your sleeping quarters."

"You assume I don't know where I'm going."

She whispered, "You've been a little confused today. I didn't tell the others." She led him up the stairs and down to the end of the hall. "Here you go." She opened the door to a huge room. A chandelier hung over the large bed.

"Thank you, Camella."

"Will you be needing company tonight, Sir?"

He shook his head, stunned. "Do I normally need company?"

She let go a nervous laugh. "No, but I'm worried about you. You don't seem yourself today."

"I think I'll be all right."

"Very well, goodnight, Sir." She walked out and pulled the doors closed.

What was that all about? Morgan opened his closet. Thirty designer suits hung in a row, with numerous shirts. A row of nearly identical, except for the color, shoes sat on the floor. He picked each one up and checked the bottom of them. *None of these have been worn.* Looking in the mirror he examined his face. *Who are you? You're not who they think you are.* There were recent scissor marks in his salt and pepper hair. His skin around his eyes was tanned, but not as much around his mouth. *I had a beard recently.*

Sitting down on the bed, he pulled off his shoes. There was no big toenail on his left foot. *There's a story there. I wonder what it is.* Taking a deep breath, Morgan thought, *why am I looking a gift horse in the mouth? I'm in a fancy house with servants all around. Why not just go with it?* He took off his shirt then stood up and stared at himself in the mirror again. *This isn't my life. I want my life back, whatever that is.*

He crawled into the bed. The satin sheets made him feel like he was going to slide off of it if he moved too fast. Forgetting his problems, he fell asleep.

Light flooded the room. Morgan sat up in bed. The butler stood at the foot of it. "Good morning, Sir. The office called. Your flight has been moved up a day. Your bags are packed, and the car is waiting for you.

You just have time for breakfast. I've laid out your clothes at the foot of the bed. I'll let you get dressed."

"Where am I going?"

"Istanbul again."

Again? He waited for the butler to leave the room before getting out of bed and into his clothes. *Why can't I remember anything?*

He headed downstairs, ate up his breakfast, and then headed towards the car. He passed Camella in the hall. She wasn't smiling. *What is that look? Sympathy or fear?* he wondered.

"I have a note from the big boss." Charles handed it to Morgan.

Morgan, the papers Mr. Kucuk needs to sign are in your briefcase. Don't come back until he signs them. - Jack-

Morgan leaned back in his chair. "Marty still under the weather?"

"Who?" Charles asked.

"Marty, my regular driver."

"Oh, yeah, Marty. Um, he's very sick. I'll be around for a while."

"Uh, huh." Morgan shook his head.

Instead of pulling into a major airport, the car parked in front of a small airport on the outskirts of the city. Charles led Morgan through the building and out onto the tarmac to the waiting plane. The pilot and co-pilot stood at the base of the stairs.

"Good morning, Mr. Percy. As soon as you get on board, we'll be on our way," the pilot said.

"Oh, I forgot my suitcase."

"It's already on the plane, Sir."

Morgan looked at the pilot and then at Charles. He hadn't seen anyone lug his bag between the car and the plane. "Oh, okay. I guess I'm ready then."

"Very good, climb on up."

Morgan walked up the stairs and into the roomy interior of the plane. It had eight plush seats, each one by an oversized window. He sat down and the copilot came into the cabin. "We have no steward, so I have to do double duty. I have coffee or hot cocoa, or you can have a cold soda. We also have food. Here is a list of items. Let me know when you want something, and I'll get it."

"I'm okay for now. I just had breakfast."

"True, but it's going to be a long flight."

Morgan nodded. "How long will it be?"

"It's a twelve-hour flight, but we'll be going through ten time zones, so we won't be getting there until late tomorrow afternoon. It will be the next day before you'll meet with whoever they have you set up with."

"I'm having problems with my memory. Do I take this trip often?"

"People from your company do. I haven't seen you before, but they could be also contracting with another flight service. I don't know."

"Thank you."

It was a long flight, but the ability to get up and walk around helped Morgan get through it. Darkness had fallen by the time the plane landed. A car pulled up as soon as he stepped out of the plane. His luggage was put in the back of it while a man escorted him through customs. With a rubber stamp in his passport, the limo whisked him off to a five-star hotel.

The suitcase contents were put in drawers for him, and the bed turned down by the bellhop. Morgan didn't question anything. Exhausted, he slipped into bed.

Breakfast arrived within minutes of him waking up. He sat on the edge of the bed and ate the eggs, toast, and potatoes then dressed. A few minutes later, a man in a black suit escorted him to the car and off to a large ornate building directly on the Bosphorus Strait. Morgan watched as ship after ship went by on their way to the Mediterranean Ocean or the Black Sea.

Two large doors opened and a man with black hair and a thin mustache stepped out. "Mr. Percy, how good to see you. Come in."

The man pointed to a chair and Morgan sat down. "You must be Kucuk. I have some papers for you to sign."

"Of course, I'm Mr. Kucuk. How can you have forgotten about me after all your visits?"

"I apologize." Morgan sat the papers on the table and Mr. Kucuk signed them without another word.

"There you go. Do you have time to see some of the sights of our wonderful city or do you have to rush back again?"

"I'm afraid I don't have control over my schedule."

"You have my phone number. Let me know when you get your schedule sorted out." Kucuk stood up and showed him the door.

That was brief. Back down at the car, the driver drove him back to the hotel without another word. He found his suitcase already packed and a sack lunch waiting for him. He Sat down to eat. As he did another man came into the room and grabbed his suitcase. "Your driver is waiting."

The driver took him back to the same airport he had come in on. This time instead of him being the only passenger waiting, a long line of people filled the room. The driver had brought his bag in and stood in line behind him. As he looked up, he saw the Customs agent staring at him. The agent's eyes widened as he looked over to three men and a dog standing at the front of the line and then back at him.

The three men moved down the line. The dog sniffed each person as it passed. Morgan turned to say something to the driver. The man and the suitcase had disappeared. *This can't be good.* As the dog sniffed Morgan's pants leg, it sat down.

"Take him," a gruff voice said. Hands grabbed both of Morgan's arms and the next thing he knew, he sat across the desk from a man in uniform. "Where are the drugs?"

Morgan trembled inside, but then shrugged and said, "I don't know about any drugs."

The man bellowed, getting so close to Morgan that he could smell the man's bad breath. "I know you have drugs, the dog alerted on you. Stop playing stupid and tell me where they are."

"I'm telling you the truth."

"Where is your suitcase, Mr.—" checking the name on the passport, "—Morgan."

"I travel light."

Two hours later a disheveled Morgan stepped onto the plane.

"We didn't think you were going to make it," the copilot said as he handed Morgan a coffee.

"They strip-searched me."

"Yes, those Turks can be brutal. It's all over now. We'll have you home as soon as possible."

When he arrived back in the United States, Morgan made his way to the car. He hadn't slept a wink on the way back. The interrogation had played over and over in his mind. "We'll be waiting for you next time. We'll know you're coming and catch you red-handed with the drugs. You're going to prison if you try again," were the man's departing words, as he handed Morgan's passport back.

When Charles picked him up, he apologized. "I have to stop and get gas. I didn't notice the tank was empty." As they pulled into the gas station, Morgan stepped out of the car to stretch his legs.

"J.J. is that you?"

Morgan turned to see an old, short, grey-haired man with a bushy beard.

"Phil?" *How do I know his name?*

"I almost didn't recognize you without your beard."

Charles stepped between them. "Leave us alone you panhandler." He pushed Phil. Phil tripped and landed backward in a bush. "We need to go, now." Charles shoved Morgan back into the car and drove off.

Morgan didn't stop, but walked straight up the stairs, took a shower, and slid into bed. An hour later, the butler opened the curtains to let light stream into the room. "Jack wants to see you."

Jack, the head of this organization. Morgan dressed and headed downstairs. There in the dining room were four men in tailored three-piece suits standing next to the table.

Morgan folded his arms. "You had me smuggling drugs into Turkey."

Jack smiled. "Yes, cocaine in and opium out. Over the short time you were there you handled six and a half million in drugs."

"Except the opium didn't make it out. They turned around at the airport," Morgan replied.

"Not true. While the authorities were busy with you, we took it through the back gate, with a little help from the customs agent we own. Before you checked in to my rehab center, you were just another drunken bum. We cleaned you up and gave you all this." Jack nodded to Camilla, and she dragged a trash can into the room. "Supper's ready. I threw my half-eaten hamburger in there along with some cold fries. That's what you're used to, isn't it?"

Morgan ignored the gesture. "You stole my memory."

"It's not a bad thing. Joey James. I think you should thank me for giving you a lot better name than that. What type of mother would name you Joey James? I know, the same type of mother who would die of a drug overdose four years later sending you to foster care for the rest of your childhood. The doctor told me we could implant new memories into your head after giving you the drug, but that didn't work. You questioned everything from day one. No matter, I'm

192

offering to keep you on anyway. You did a great job of getting through airport security even when you were detained. You can have three meals a day, stay in the house, and even have female companionship any time you want it. All I ask is you make a trip once a week or so."

Camella blushed when Morgan glanced over at her. He faced James again. "I see, and if I say no?"

"That would be very unhealthy."

"Having no real option, I guess I'm in." Morgan swallowed.

"Great. Take the rest of the week off. I'll send you on another trip on Monday."

Morgan scowled as Jack and his henchmen left. The cook came out. "Let's get you some real food. Camella, get that trash can out of here. Have a seat, Morgan. I'll whip you up something nice."

"Thanks."

When Camella came back in, the cook set three servings of lamb chops and fried potatoes on the table. The two of them joined Morgan for dinner.

"They are terrible people, manipulating lives as they do," the cook complained.

"Shh," Camella put her finger to her lips then whispered, "They'll hear you."

"I don't care. Nobody else would take this thankless job." She ate another spoonful of potatoes.

Morgan scanned the room for cameras and microphones. He knew they were there but couldn't see any. "Were there others before me?"

"Yes, they enjoy their life here until they get caught, then we get another one," the cook replied.

After dinner, Morgan headed straight up to bed. A few minutes after lying down he felt Camella's hand rubbing his back. "I hope you're doing okay."

He grabbed her wrist and pulled her onto the bed then threw the covers over both of them. Whispering he asked, "Do you know where the cameras are?"

"Yes. They take turns monitoring them. There's one pointed towards the door in this room, but you can also see the bed on it. There are also cameras in the main hall, the dining room, the study, and the living room."

"How about the yard?"

"The back and the front, nothing on the sides."

"Who is monitoring them tonight?"

"No one monitors them this late. The cook goes home, only I and the butler live in the building. Everything is recorded though."

"Can you disable the camera in this room?"

She slipped off her skirt and blouse. "I have to make them think I have a good reason to turn it off." Getting out of bed, she walked up to the camera and switched it off. "There."

Morgan jumped out of bed and ran to the window.

"No, not that one," Camella said. "This one. Run straight out and don't turn until you're in the neighbor's front yard."

He slid the window open, and let himself down, then vanished into the night.

Jack reviewed the surveillance video, rewound it, and watched it again. "Camella forgot to turn the camera back on. At least he had some fun his last night here."

"Do we go after him?" Charles asked.

"Nah. We'll let him go back to eating out of trash cans. Another candidate just checked into our rehab center. The doctor says he'll be a good match for the brain-altering drug. We'll get him cleaned up and start over."

Morgan sniffed. He had never noticed the bad smell coming from under the freeway before. A few tents lay in the middle of scattered debris. Then he spotted his friend.

"J.J., You're back," Phil said.

"I'm only here for a visit. I've contacted my daughter in the Midwest. When I told her, I was clean and sober she said I could come back until I get my feet under me. Her mother raised her to hate me, so she's got a lot of issues. It was a huge thing for her to do."

"I thought I lost my best buddy when you checked into that rehab center. Now I'm going to lose you again."

"I'm going on to a better life. You should try it."

"I'm too old." Phil shook his head. "Used to be you didn't mind this life. Are your memories coming back?"

"Mostly. I'll be all right, my friend. I'm off the booze, but I have a long bus ride ahead of me. I've got to go."

"Good luck. If you fail, your tent is still here next to mine. Come back."

Morgan waved goodbye as he headed down the hill.

Clark Graham

THE CHRISTMAS STAR

With his signature fedora on his head, Albert Smith studied the plans for his kinetic light. It didn't work, at least not yet. He knew the lights worked. He had checked them out with a hand generator, but the kinetic energy source was too low in wattage to turn them on. He looked up just as his supervisor came towards him with a packet of papers. "Hello, Bill."

"Sorry, Albert, but I'm going to have to take you off of the Kinetic light project. The big boss says it's a pit where we throw money. You've been assigned to help Charles with the Delmore Project." He set the papers down on the desk.

"I have been working on this for six months now. What do I do with all the stuff left over from the Kinetic light project?"

"Scrap it."

"Can I work on it from home?"

"It's all garbage as far as the boss is concerned. Take it home if you want."

Albert smiled. "Thanks."

In his spare time, Albert worked on different ways to get the light to work using only the energy found in nature. One day, near Christmas he put the wires in an evergreen branch his wife had given him to make a wreath out of. The light didn't come on except for a faint glow. *More power, I need more power.*

He wrapped the branch in Christmas lights and plugged them in. The flow from the kinetic light shone so bright he had to turn it off. "It worked, it worked." His heart danced. There would never be a commercial application for his invention he realized, because the Kinetic energy came from the lights wrapped around the branch, not from the branch itself.

Deciding it would at least brighten his tree, he made a star out of wood, painted it white, and stapled the light strip inside of it.

"Honey," he said as he came back into the house. "Can we have a real tree this year?"

"No, we have a perfectly good artificial tree in the garage."

"I thought you wouldn't want it after the mice made a nest in it." The mice really didn't, as far as he knew, but they could have, so that was the story he went with.

"Eek," his wife said. She hated mice and everything to do with them.

With the old Christmas tree on the curb come garbage day, Albert, his dear wife, and daughter Susan made a trek to a nearby tree farm. After picking out the perfect one, they raced home. Setting up the stand he put the lights on while his wife Judy and daughter

Susan put on the ornaments. He stuck the two wire prongs into the tree itself and then turned on the lights. The star lit up to full brightness, even brighter than it did before.

"Honey," his wife said. "Can you turn that star down a bit?" Judy shielded her eyes with her hand.

"Nope, the bigger the tree, the brighter the star."

Susan, for her part, danced round, and round. "It's so beautiful. Like a real star, Daddy."

TWENTY YEARS LATER

"Where's the Christmas star, Mommy?"

Susan sighed. It was hard to explain to ten-year-old Annie about life's tragedies and how people responded to them. They hadn't even entered the house but already Susan's daughter could tell the star wasn't on.

"Honey, remember Grandma passed away. Grandpa is so sad about it; he hasn't set up a tree this year."

A tear rolled down Annie's cheek. "It's not Christmas without the star."

"Honey," Susan said, "It is still Christmas, it's just not as bright. It's not the same without Grandma." She felt a pang of guilt. Even as a toddler Annie would look up at the Christmas star and smile from ear to ear.

TEN YEARS LATER

"What are you still doing here? The snow is piling up and you need to get going before they close the passes," Susan said.

Annie had been through every box in the attic twice. "I was thinking, now that I have my own place, I want that old Christmas star that Grandpa built."

"Oh, honey, Uncle George took the Christmas boxes. I'm sure he has it."

"I'll give him a call on my way out the door."

"Uncle George, this is Annie. Do you still have the Christmas boxes that Grandpa had?"

"I'm sorry, you just missed them. I cleaned out the garage and donated everything to the thrift store. Was there something you wanted in particular?"

"I was hoping to get Grandpa's Christmas star."

"I'm sure that thing doesn't work anymore. If you hurry over to Rodger's Thrift store, they might not have sold it yet."

"I've got to get back home before the pass closes. If it isn't too much trouble, can you check to see if they, have it?"

"Sure, I'll swing by right now."

"Thanks, Uncle."

Getting dressed, George took one step out of the house. "Ugh, snow." *I'll tell her they sold it. Probably didn't work anyway.* He took off his coat and hung it back in the closet.

"What is it?" The man examined it.

"I think it's for a Christmas tree, Dad."

"Is it supposed to light up?"

"It looks like it used to. Those are only stub wires. I think the real ones were ripped out."

The father shook his head. "I don't want it then."

"I do. It's better than what I have, which is nothing."

"It's all yours then, Son."

THE NEXT CHRISTMAS

"Annie, this is Kyle. He's just started at the company, too," Scott said.

"Hello, Annie, it's good to meet you."

"It's good to meet you too." She gave him a smile.

Sitting alone at lunch, Annie gazed up from her phone to see Kyle standing there. "May I have this seat?" He asked.

"Yes, of course."

As he sat, he asked. "You're having a light lunch today."

"Oh," she said. "I didn't think I was starting today. I had expected that after the interview I would go home and wait for their answer, but they hired me on the spot. I didn't bring any cash with me."

"I can't have you starving. What can I get for you?"

"You don't have to do that, I'll be fine."

"The calzone is to die for, I hear. I'll bring you one."

She blushed. "Thank you."

The calzone hit the spot. As they chatted, they found out how much they had in common.

"I'm so far away from home, I don't even have a Christmas tree this year, but I have ornaments." Kyle said.

"I have a tree, but not many ornaments. My grandpa had the best ones, but my uncle gave them away after my grandfather died. Talk about a Scrooge."

"How about I bring my ornaments to your house, and we share a Christmas tree together? A tree won't fit in my tiny apartment anyway."

Annie thought for a second. "Why not?"

Later that night, after a nice dinner together at a restaurant, they met at Annie's house. Kyle admired the tree.

"I know, it's not a real tree. It's a hand-me-down from my uncle. He felt so bad about giving my grandfather's ornaments away that he gave me this tree." Annie said.

"I was thinking how real it looked. My father's tree doesn't even look this good."

She smiled. "Thank you. Should we get started?"

As they were decorating, she pulled out one of his ornaments and admired it.

"Grandpa used to have one like this. He would put it on the lowest branch so, when I was a baby, I could crawl over to it and chew on it. I loved blue. The funny thing is, this one has teeth marks. I must not have been the only kid who liked chewing on blue plastic ornaments."

"That's funny." He waited until all the ornaments were on the tree, then said,

"Here is my favorite thing. It's a Christmas star. It doesn't light up or anything, but it's still pretty."

When he unwrapped the newspaper from it, she burst into tears.

"What did I do? I didn't want to offend you. It's just a star."

"No, you don't understand." She held the star in her hands. "My grandfather made this. I thought it was lost, but here it is."

"Your grandfather made that? How do you know?"

"Where are the wires?"

He shook his head. "There are only two small stubs of wires. I poked them into the star."

She dug the wires out. "It does light up."

"Really?"

"Yes, but only on real trees. It works with kinetic energy somehow. It was a project he worked on long ago."

He looked up and down on the decorated tree. "I'm guessing we're going tree shopping."

She already had her phone out. "Here's a tree lot. They don't close until nine." She put her coat on and handed him his.

When they arrived back at her place, they undecorated the artificial tree and redecorated the real one. Putting the star on top, she pushed the two prongs into the bark of the tree.

He smiled, "Yes, I see it. There is a faint glow."

"You haven't seen anything yet." She crossed her fingers. "Turn on the tree's lights."

When he turned them on, the Christmas star lit up the room better than sunlight.

She gasped and pointed at the base of the tree. "Grandpa." A shadow of a man in a fedora hat was illuminated by the light. A man who wasn't there, but yet he was. After only a few seconds, the shadow faded away.

Every year, when the star lit up the room the first time that season, the shadow reappeared. A shadow of a man who wasn't there, but yet he was, would appear at the base of the tree for a few seconds. Annie and Kyle, both knew it was her grandfather looking out for them. The shadow stayed longer when the children began to arrive.

Annie also noticed that no matter where she put the blue plastic ornament, it always ended up on a bottom branch where littlest children could get to it and chew on it.

ABOUT THE AUTHOR

Clark Graham is a member of the Science Fiction and Fantasy Writers of America and has written forty books. He also has served as the president of the Skagit Valley Writer's League and a league member for the last five years. "It's been an honor to work with the amazing people of the Skagit Valley," he says. "I've learned so much from this experience."

https://www.facebook.com/Elvenshore

elvenshore@gmail.com

https://www.amazon.com/Clark-Graham/e/B008O2QYWE

Keshecolashcomak
Melba Burke

THE MIDAE DRUM

Little Bird draws his father's hunting rifle from the corner in the kitchen and checks the chamber. He takes one last look at his mother Adeline, a Turtle Mountain Chippewa, and heads toward the oak grove above the slough seeking solitude. His mother's unwise choice in choosing a French mate has become clearer to him the older he grows and is the worry that drives him to hunt alone today.

Concealed in the trees alongside a game trail, Little Bird thinks about how his mother's band of Chippewa were driven out of their homeland by settlers wanting free land made possible through the passage of the Homestead Act. How at sixteen his mother and her father were forced to migrate from the region of the great lakes, across Minnesota, and into North Dakota where they made their home on Turtle Mountain.

He has lived on Turtle Mountain all his life. The Reservation of 1933 is nothing like the Madeline Island of 1891 where she grew up; nor is it like the Indian territories of Minnesota or Wisconsin that his mother described as part of her journey west.

He is thankful that she shared her Indian ways with him, showing him where to find healing plants, teaching him to track animals, and build shelters to protect himself from the elements. But best of all, he likes that she shared the sacred rites of the *Midewiwin* with him. Taught him to break the bonds of the physical world, change shape, and enter the spirit world like his ancestors.

When younger, he and his father butted heads because he refused to attend a missionary school like his half-brothers and sisters did before him. More recently, a day or two ago, he refused to go to church wanting to enter the sweat lodge instead. That was when his father said to him, "Roderick," using his white name, "the sweat lodge and the *Midewiwin* are little more than witchcraft."

Stung by his father's words Little Bird had lashed out, "I don't like your Church with its rattle of rosary beads and threats of burning in Hell!" To make matters worse he yelled, "I like *Midewiwin*. I'm not going to Church I'm going to the sweat lodge." His outburst severed their bond. They went their separate ways, he back to the company of his mother and his father to longer work days.

For a long time, he was satisfied working beside his father clearing their farmland, raising cattle, caring for horses, and building houses like the men in the white settlements. All that changed for him when he sought employment and discovered being a mixed blood limited his chance of making a living at anything other than being a field hand.

Now at the age of sixteen, he feels trapped between two parents who are so different from each other they refuse to speak even the same language. Sure, he speaks both their languages fluently and often translates for them. Of late, even that has gone by the wayside. And now, here on the hill overlooking the slough, he realizes that both his homelife and the prospect for any kind of life off the reservation, for him, is bleak.

A whitetail deer moves into the clearing interrupting his thoughts. He puts the bead of the rifle on it and waits for it to turn.

" Little Bird."

Hearing his mother call his name, startles him. His finger twitches and the gun fires. The bullet strikes a tree, and the deer bounds off. Little Bird grunts his displeasure. Wasting bullets is frowned upon by both his parents. Retracing his steps, he heads toward the sound of his mother's voice.

Adeline is waiting for him on a grassy knoll filled with the pungent odor of sweet grass overlooking the garden. A red-tail hawk is circling above her. She pats the ground next to her inviting him to sit. "The hawk, Little Bird," she gestures toward it "foretells the coming of, a battle." His mother's soft voice is so different from the sharp nasal French of his father, Edmond, sure to be upset he shot the gun and spent a bullet needlessly.

He settles in beside Adeline preferring to be by her side while she finishes the willow basket she is weaving, then face the consequence with his father, for a failed hunt.

"I heard you fire the gun." Adeline crinkles her nose.

"I missed."

"Dad won't like that."

"What do you think he'll do to me?"

"Do to you? You worry too much." Adeline sets the basket aside. "I called you here to tell you a story about the Midae drum which your grandfather on my side, the Indian side of the family, told me."

"What's a Midae drum?"

"It's a water drum made from the trunk of a basswood tree and is used in the awakening ceremony of the Midewiwin."

He looks at his mother, who has not shared her wisdom with him for a long while and wonders why she chose to do so today.

Adeline closes her eyes, presses her hands together, and begins to speak in her native tongue. "One day your grandfather heard the thump of the *Midae* drum. When he walked in its direction, The rhythmic beat of the drum grew louder. It led him to Turtle Island where our Tribe's creation story takes place. Masked in warpaint the colors of fire and water a warrior stood armed for battle, opposite him on the island.

The warrior raised his club, challenging your grandfather. Your grandfather charged. He and the warrior fought long and hard for three days. Upon his return to the village, your grandfather shared his story with his clan and a feast was held in his honor. He later became a war chief, fought the Sioux, and extended our homeland into their territory."

Impressed with the outcome of his grandfather's battle he wonders what would happen if he were to fight with his father. Pushing that idea aside, instead Little Bird says, "perhaps it's time for me to heed the call of the *Midae* drum." '

Adeline nods. "Perhaps."

Her voice softens, "When you hear the *Midae* drum, you must follow its sound east to Turtle Island, like your grandfather did. There you will find a warrior whom you must fight, if you are defeated you will not return."

"Will not return?" He glances away and shudders.

She turns to him. "If you fight bravely, you will find your place among our people and your path in life."

"Where is this. . .this Turtle Island?"

"The drum will show you the way. Follow its sound."

When the sun dips under the horizon, and the moon shows amid the stars announcing the appearance of the elders in the spirit world above them, they gather their things together and walk toward home.

Little Bird chooses not to tell his father about missing the deer.

Edmond notices he has one less bullet and frowns.

For many moons, Little Bird listens for the beat of the *Midae* drum. Nothing happens and Little Bird stops listening. His mother's story is forgotten.

One morning at dawn, Little Bird is standing amid lime-green leaves that shimmer where dew moistens the carpet of decay beneath his bare feet, and brown leaves and white cottonwood down press into the earth. Abruptly, the water of the slough vibrates. He focuses, looking for a disturbance. He hears a rhythmic thumping. It's a drum, he realizes, a water drum.

As if they too are familiar with the rhythmic beat of the drum though unaware of its meaning, the eared grebe, meadowlark, and redwing blackbird sing giving tribute to the sun's first rays. Muskrats lie on fallen logs bleached white from years of sun-scorched days. Cattails, ripe and full, sway on sharp green shafts as the breeze sweeps over the marsh where water striders tread and minnows dart to the surface to feed.

The yellow, amid the light brown of his eyes, darts, hawklike, this way and that in search of the sound's origin. He waits. Listens. And shivers not from the cold but from the memory of his grandfather's battle with the warrior, his possible fate maybe even his death, which now lies before him.

The drum beat increases, drawing Little Bird from the trees into the sunlight. He laps water beside a coyote pup and drinks his fill before rising to gathers nuts, roots, and berries, and places them in his pouch in preparation for his journey.

The shadow of a red-tail hawk circles over the grassland, where the jackrabbits feed. It circles over him, silhouetted against the morning sun. Watching it, he remembers the omen foretelling a battle, his battle with a warrior.

A feather drops from the hawk, and he catches it in the palm of his hand, makes a small braid in his hair, and ties the feather to it with a narrow strip of red cloth that floats above his black locks. He sprinkles tobacco on the ground and gives thanks to Grandfather, the uncreated spirit *Kizhi Manido* for this gift.

He carves a warclub to fit his hand and looks eastward in anticipation of his journey. Born to run, Little Bird catches his stride quickly. He nourishes his body while he runs and stops only to drink. Like his grandfather before him, he knows only that he is being called and without hesitation he must follow the sound of the drum.

Bare legs blending with the browns of the open terrain, he moves at an ever-quickening pace, following the rhythmic thump of the *Midae* drum. He runs past beaver dams, leaps over fallen aspens and willows pushed on by the wind. Through the day he runs, his broad shoulders churn with the sway of his body, his shadow shortens and lengthens as the sun moves across the sky. Onward beyond the pain of endurance and muscle fatigue, he runs in pursuit of his destiny. Into the night he runs in moonlit shadows searching for the warrior of Turtle Island.

From the dark forest of night, he emerges into the light as the morning sun rises in the eastern sky. Over the cracked earth of the hot open prairie he runs, past the ring-necked pheasant strutting its golden-brown body; past a red headed woodpecker whose rat, tat, tat, competes with the thump of the Midae drum. Through the grasslands of the mule deer, into the cool of the hill country home of the wolf, and prowling cougar he runs. In acceptance of whatever lies ahead he presses on.

He beats the air with the war club clutched in his hand, as the beat of the drum drives him on. He is hot and hungry, bruised and aching as he journeys over mother earth.

After a while, fatigue overtakes him, and time begins to slow for Little Bird. On day three he enters the spirit world where the four *Wabununk' daci,' Midae manido,* merge from the four points of the compass. Into his medicine bag he places the life-giving breath of each.

The "*Wa, hi, hi, hi,*" the song of the East spirit from the land of his mother's childhood, calls out to him. He floats toward her through the splendid colors of vermilion and blue that fills the sky. Across his face and forehead, the *Manido* streaks alternating colors of red and blue, preparing him for battle.

At dusk a great lake appears and in its center is Turtle Island. The strike of the *Midae* drum like thunder rolls across the sky. Upon reaching the water's edge, from his hair he pulls the hawk's feather and lays it on the water. Its magic carries him to the island where he lights the sacred fire.

The ancestors appear in the night sky above him, he circles the sacred fire and sings the "*Wa, hi, hi, hi,*" his death song, for knows he may not live past this day.

From his medicine bag, Little Bird pulls sacred tobacco and sprinkles it into the fire.

Out of the fire leaps a warrior. The warrior is agile and muscular with streaks of resplendent vermilion and blue, across his face, and forehead. The warrior's up-raised warclub casts an ominous shadow across Little Bird's heart. So close in manner and appearance is the warrior to Little Bird, that the one could pass for the other.

"If I were to reach out, I feel I would be reaching toward myself." Little Bird whispers.

Wasting no time, the two warriors charge, war clubs clash breaking the silence. The sound reverberates across the island, sparks fly overhead and rain down upon them. The warrior's eyes flash as he blocks Little Bird's advance and lightning-quick, sweeps him off his feet, and lifts his club to strike.

Little Bird rolls out of reach and springs to his feet. Blow after mighty blow is struck in their deadly dance. The sky turns to blue-black with streaks of fire-red blocking the ancestors from Little Bird's view. Flashes of lightning rip through the sky and strike the earth. Rumbles shake the island.

The cougar and the wolf leap out of the darkness drawn by the smell of Blood. Now prey, the warriors turn and make quick work of the predators. The battle rages on throughout the night.

By morning the clouds are swept away and Daylight breaks blinding the warrior. Seizing the moment Little Bird strikes a fatal blow. The beat of the *Midae* drum quiets. An ache engulfs Little Bird as if it is he who lies crumpled on the ground.

He lays the fallen warrior near the sacred fire mourning the sad memory of his severed bond with his father. From his medicine bag he takes life preserving plants and treats the warrior's wounds. In so doing, he realizes there is a likeness of himself as well as that of his father in the warrior's appearance but can see no difference between his Indian heritage and the French part of him.

Into his medicine bag he reaches for the breaths of the four *Midae Manido*, grasping the breaths firmly in his hands, he circles the corpse four times. With each circle, he, blows the breath of one of the *Midae Manido* into the warrior.

The Midae drum sounds, deep within the warrior and he awakens. "*Wa, hi, hi, hi.*" they sing and merge. The separate traditions of his mother and father meld within him. Now, he is neither a French man nor an Indian. He is, for the first time himself. Accepting his new identity, he is ready to take his place among his people and accept his path.

When his feet touch the ground, the earth once again smells of sweetgrass.

ABOUT THE AUTHOR

Melba Burke is a Chippewa from Turtle Mountain in North Dakota. She received her Indian Name *Keshecolashcomak,* Clear-of-the-Moon, from her uncle, Young Charlie Cree born in 1895.The Midae Drum is a story selection from her historical novel in process. You may contact her at melbaburke47@gmail.com

Joseph A. Vitovec

THE HOME COMING

The lights of the coast fell away, and the whine of the Lufthansa Boeing 747's powerful engines dropped a notch as the plane settled into its cruising speed and turned eastward toward the great void of darkness that was the Atlantic. Jan Neuman slouched in his seat, eyes closed, but sleep was out of the question. If anything, he felt a touch of nausea. His mind reeled. It was all so far-fetched, so unimaginable—so incredible! Going home. After forty years, going home! Just the thought gave him the shakes.

The young woman in the seat next to him stirred and yawned. Their eyes met, and he gave her an encouraging smile. "Long night," he said.

She blushed. "It's my first trip overseas. Are you German?" She evidently noted his accent.

He shook his head. "American...but I was born in Czechoslovakia. And you?"

"I'm from Austin. Got a job teaching at the American High School in Wiesbaden. Don't speak German; don't know anything about Germany." She smiled timidly. "Is it— "

"You'll like it. It's all modern now, not what it used to be...what it was like when I first saw it back in forty-eight."

"Forty-eight? That's— "

"Forty years. Forty years ago. Before you were born, I'm sure."

She considered his answer and puckered her brow. "You said you were born in former Yugoslavia— "

"Czechoslovakia," he corrected her, soothing her embarrassment with a smile. "I was a student back then...probably younger than you are now...and an activist, you might say...political activist. There was a coup, an overthrow of our government by the Communists, and I would have been jailed if I'd stayed—so I escaped into Germany. Spent a couple of years in refugee camps; was fortunate to immigrate to America."

She looked at him quizzically. "So why are you flying to Germany?"

"You know, the Cold War's over; the regime at home has changed. So, I thought I'd go back and see, retrace my steps. Close the circle, so to speak."

Jan had never expected to return home at all. For all these years, the communist regime in his homeland seemed as solid and impenetrable as the Iron Curtain that shrouded it. Home, when he thought of it at all, had become but a wisp of nostalgia—a set of static images bleached sepia by time. Long ago, he had resigned himself to Fate, the great unpredictable mover

220

that had toyed with him and shaped his life in ways he could have never imagined.

The young woman next to him fell asleep, and he himself did not know when he finally drifted off or how long he had slept, but he woke up with a start as the plane dipped in altitude. He pressed his face against the window and watched as the countryside below him rose as if to greet him. He knew his coming was an impulsive act—now that he had had a little time to reflect, sober thoughts intruded. What would he find? His parents were dead, his family gone. There would be no one to greet him. Still, the desire was overpowering, almost primeval, like that of migrating birds that travel thousands of miles to the places of their birth, or like the salmon that brave countless dangers to reach the headwaters of their origin, only to die.

The plane landed with a thump and taxied to the Frankfurt terminal. The young woman wished him luck (he realized he never knew her name) and disappeared with the Army escort who met her at the gate. By the time he cleared Customs and picked up the rental, a small Ford, the lights in the great bustling city were coming on. There was no point going any further tonight. He found a Novotel near the autobahn and, letting go of all his emotions, tired to the bone, fell into a dreamless death-like sleep.

The rolling countryside around Regensburg was just as he remembered, a checkerboard of raw-earth fields emerging from their wintry slumber. Yet, the city itself had changed. In place of the piles of rubble and bleak streets he had once wandered after his harrowing escape, it was now a vibrant and thriving metropolis. No traces of the Goethe Strasse camp where he had spent the first days of his exile, but a modern school alive with children's voices. The ghosts of the past were gone. He drove on, thinking fleetingly about the wizened

German farmer and his family in the mountains who took him in as he ran for his life under a hail of bullets following the communist coup d'état in 'forty-eight. Perhaps they, too, were gone. All the relics of those times had vanished—now he, Jan, felt like the relic.

The sun was high in the sky when he finally reached the border. The single German customs man waved him off when he tried to hand him his passport, but a passel of guards spilled from a lichen-covered bunker when he reached the Czech side. His heart fluttered as he passed under his country's flag – his flag – swaying in the breeze over the roadway.

"Halt! Documents!" One of the guards stepped into the road with his arm raised, while the others just stood there, glaring at him with mistrust. He could see it in their eyes.

Jan handed him his passport as his mind reeled. Dressed in Russian-style uniforms, looking surly under their saucer-like hats, the guards eyed him with a frosty stare. *Only a few weeks ago, they'd probably have gladly put a bullet through me,* he reflected, a chill crawling up his spine.

"American, huh?" The guard gave him a sneer.

"A Czech. I'm Czech. I was born here—"

"American. It says American here," the guard cut him off. "Where are you going?"

"Čekaná."

"Čekaná? Why Čekaná?" The guard raised his eyebrows.

"It's my home. I was born there," Jan retorted.

"Number? Address?"

Jan suddenly realized that he no longer had one—that he no longer *had* a home. He shrugged.

"When you get there, you must register at the District office, understand? Within two days."

"Yes, of course," Jan replied in Czech.

Surprised, the guard gave him an amused look. "So, you still speak the language, eh? You speak with a foreign accent." He chortled.

Suppressing his chagrin, Jan gave him an uneasy smile.

"What's in the bag?"

"Just personal stuff."

"Open it."

Jan opened his suitcase and the guard poked in it before letting the lid down with a grunt. "Forty dollars. Every foreigner must pay forty dollars."

Smirking, the guard pocketed the money and lazily touched the bill of his hat with two fingers in a salute as Jan drove away from the guardhouse, followed by the glare of half a dozen condescending eyes.

The highway ahead was rutted. Passing a gaping scar bulldozed into the undulating landscape, dotted with vast piles of wire fence and concertina wire, and remnants of what he guessed had been guard towers, Jan realized that these were what was left of the electrified barrier that was the Iron Curtain, designed to keep the "enemy" out and the people like him in. *Until a few weeks ago, I was the enemy,* he mused.

It was late in the afternoon when he finally reached the turn where the road dipped into the valley and stretched, arrow-like, under a swaying canopy of poplars, toward his town. Shivering with excitement, he felt his chest tighten as he rode down the familiar street. And then there it was—his house, his home, incredibly just like the day he left: the same pink stucco with white trim and red-tiled roof, and geranium boxes in the windows, and the gate and the cobblestone passageway. Everything. It was all there. Untouched. Nothing had changed. Nothing! The sight overwhelmed him. *Was he dreaming? Had his memory been playing a trick on him?* Light-headed and flushed all over, he looked around in disbelief—and then he panicked. Feeling suddenly like an interloper, he gunned the motor and, spinning the wheels of the little Ford in the loose gravel, took off, driving randomly through town, past familiar sights, past the river where he'd fished for trout, no longer a frolicking stream but a muddy rivulet full of slimy algae; past the silo near the railroad station, still speckled with bullet holes from the strafing by the American P-38's he'd survived back in forty-five; past the old synagogue, now a hollow decaying ruin with its windows knocked out and roof caving in; past the square, now shabby under the perpetually resplendent canopy of lindens. It was all there, precisely as he remembered; everything—except one thing: The deserted streets had a decaying feeling about them. It was as though life had gone out of his town.

Finally, he pulled up at his house again and stepped out. He thought he saw a curtain move. The door in the house next to his creaked open, and a wizened old man ambled out. "Are you looking for someone?" he said, measuring Jan suspiciously.

Relieved to see a face, Jan smiled. "I used to live here," he said.

"Here? You used to live here?" The man's face screwed in astonishment, and he rubbed his eyes a couple of times before returning his glare to Jan. "You wouldn't be then—"

"Jan Neuman. I used to live here. I was born here. This was my home."

The man swallowed hard a couple of times. "Then you remember me. I am Zdeněk. Or maybe you don't remember?" He looked at Jan skeptically. "We went to grade school together when we were kids—remember?" He gave a short, wheezing laugh and shook his head in mock disbelief. "Jan Neuman. Jan Neu-man. Who would have thought?" He scowled. "But you're a little late."

"Zdeněk?" For a moment, Jan was taken aback, unable to accept in his mind the wreck of a man before him as his peer. Time had not been kind to him—he was aged beyond his years. But his disdainful look and acrid words stung.

"What can I say? I know, but I couldn't—" he blurted out, but Zdeněk didn't let him finish.

"You know your old man was jailed after you left? Came back broken. Sure, could've used you here. Lived there all alone. I watched him every day. In the end, couldn't even walk, take care of himself. Couldn't do anything for himself."

"I told you I couldn't—"

"Yeah!" Zdeněk looked at him sourly.

"Couldn't you—wasn't there someone who would...who could have helped? I couldn't—"

"Helped?" He laughed again and spat in the dust. "You don't understand. Nobody would even speak to him, much less help him. Because of you. He was watched. He was treated like a leper. People were afraid. He suffered while you were out there in America,

225

living it up like a king." He almost spat out the last words.

Jan felt a mixture of anger and guilt well up in him. He wanted to shout, *what right do you have,* but instead managed only a forced laugh. "Living like a king, you say? You have no idea—"

"He sure could've used you. If more of you had stayed behind, things could have been different sooner. It all could've ended—"

Though seething inside, Jan didn't want to be drawn into an argument. "I really don't know what I could have done—you know what they would've done to me. I don't want to argue with you, but—"

Just then, a young blue-eyed, flaxen-haired, pink-cheeked girl ran out of Jan's house into the street, stopped short, and gawked at them with childish curiosity.

The curtain moved again, and moments later, a young disheveled swarthy man rushed out into the street. "Alenka! Get back in! What did I tell you—" He stopped short when he noticed Jan. "Forgive her, but she is a precocious child. She shouldn't have— Alenka. Alenka! Inside, I said, or—"

"Excuse me," Jan said, "my name is Jan Neuman, and I used to live in that house."

Surprised, the man looked at him in disbelief. "You...you used to live *here*?"

"Yeah, Frank, years ago," Zdeněk cut in. "He's been gone forty years. That's Jan Neuman, old man Neuman's son. From America."

The man continued to gape at Jan as though he were an apparition.

Suddenly, Jan felt cotton mouthed. His throat was dry. He wished he were somewhere else. Finally, he summoned his courage. "I wonder if you would mind if I might step inside? Just for a few minutes, you understand; just to see, if you don't mind. I don't want to impose—"

Without changing expression, the man shrugged, uttered a single word, "Please," nodded silently to Zdeněk, and turned to the house.

The familiar echo of the slate-tiled hallway brought back a fresh flood of memories as Jan followed the man into what used to be the workroom, his parents' domain, around which his life had revolved, now transformed into a great room, with a green ceramic-tiled stove in one corner and a large table in the center. It was nothing like he remembered, nothing like the image burnt into his mind all these years. Only the clock was still there – his father's clock – ticking away loudly, measuring time with a deliberate pace. A young blond blue-eyed woman sat on a faded sofa, breastfeeding a baby. He felt a rising flood of resentment toward these strangers (*squatters* flashed through his mind), for robbing him of his dream, for usurping one of his long-cherished memories.

"This is Mr. Neuman from America," the man said. "This is Věra, my wife, and little Sláva. You already saw Alenka. I am Frank, Frank Vondra."

Blushing, the woman gently pushed away the baby, covered her bosom, stood up, and extended her hand. "Jesus Mary, is it possible? An American? From America?"

Overcoming his chagrin, Jan managed a smile. "I saw the Prague demonstrations on television...the crowds on Wenceslaus Square...the flags—. I never thought it would happen. I came back as soon as I could."

She offered him a seat and looked at him tensely.

"He says he used to live here. He wants to see the house," the husband said.

The blood drained from her face.

Trailed by the little girl, offering only cursory comments but watching him hawkishly, the woman led him through the familiar rooms, the courtyard, and the garden. There were changes, to be sure: the washroom had become an indoor toilet; the pump in the garden was gone, replaced by a spigot inside; the goat shed had become a storage shed; the orchard, his father's pride, had turned into a twisted, unkempt jungle of broken trees.

"That's not ours. The State owns it. They used to graze goats in there until last year," she said, seeing his sour look.

"How long have you been living here now?" Jan asked.

"Six years, come next month. "The State took over the house after old man…" She caught herself and blushed. "Sorry, after your father died." We were lucky to get it. They wouldn't let anyone have it unless they belonged to the Party." Embarrassed, she stopped abruptly, realizing she had misspoken.

Jan remained silent.

"We had to belong…everybody had to belong. You couldn't live if you didn't belong. We weren't really political or anything. We had to survive—"

"I understand." Jan shrugged. Doesn't matter."
He looked at his watch. It was five-thirty, and he was
getting hungry. "I guess I better go and see if I can find
a hotel for the night. It's getting late." He suddenly felt
anxious and out of place.

She smiled sadly. "There isn't anything in town.
There used to be one, but—" She fell silent for a
moment. "If you're not too fussy, you're welcome to
have supper with us and stay the night. There's a small
room upstairs, a spare. Nothing fancy, just a bed. I
know Frank wouldn't mind—"

She finally broached the subject after supper.
Jan sensed stiffness in her demeanor and
apprehension in her voice. "If this is your house, are you
going to ask us to leave?" she said.

The room suddenly became airless, oppressive.
Only the soft whimpers of the baby in her arms and the
ticking of the clock on the wall interrupted the silence.
Frank looked into his plate, but her eyes were on him,
clung to him, full of fear and despair, beginning to tear.

The question pierced a wall, releasing a flood of
realities he never thought he'd have to face. Suddenly,
he felt like an intruder. In his own home, he felt like an
intruder! Choking on feeling, he returned the woman's
look, shook his head, and looked away.

They didn't talk much after that. It was as
though a void, a remoteness, had suddenly sprung
between them. She led him to the room upstairs. It
was his old room. Even his old bed was still there, with
its straw mattress and creaky boards. He didn't sleep
well.

In the morning, after a breakfast of black bread
and strong coffee and awkward conversation, he
thanked them and walked out into the crisp air. The
streets were still devoid of life. He drove to the
cemetery and found the family grave. Not particularly

religious, more a seeker than a believer, he nevertheless stood by the cold slab of marble and prayed.

Walking down from the cemetery to where he had left his car, he stopped on the weathered granite steps under a crucifix that had been there since long before he was born and looked down on his town. It was there just as it had always been—a stage upon which a drama had just been played.

His heart ached as he took in the view. He felt alone, painfully alone—a solitary actor clinging to his imaginary spot long after the play had ended, the audience gone, the applause only an echo in the recesses of his mind. Only the props remained, vibrant but spiritless, and the mustiness so characteristic of stages—a strange mixture of antiquity and nostalgia. Somewhere along the way, he had missed his cue. The play was over. He no longer belonged.

He got into his car, drove down to the highway, and, without looking back, turned westward toward Germany for his flight home.

ABOUT THE AUTHOR

Joe Vitovec was born in Czechoslovakia. As a young man, he saw his country overran by the Germans during World War II, liberated by the Americans and Russians in 1945, and taken over by the Communists in a coup in 1948. Fear of arrest because of political activity led him to escape the regime. As a refugee, he spent more than two years in DP camps before immigration in the USA, where he made the US Air Force his career. He has degree in History from Texas Christian University and master's degree in Urban Studies from the University of Texas. He also instructed political science at the Tarrant Community College in Fort Worth, Texas. He is the award-winning author of the historical novel FULL CIRCLE. He and his wife Ruth currently reside in Anacortes, Washington.

Guy Stickney

YOU'RE OUTSIDE THE BOX, YOU'RE INSIDE THE CIRCLE

If you're outside the box, you're inside the circle
Could be a shark, could be a turtle
Life on our planet, cease to exist
If it smells like fish, eat all you wish

This is the record, that we keep for now
Show's what we do, & shows them just how
Uh, where is the cat, it followed us home
Somebody planned this, leave me alone

Looks like this guy was wrong
So, we sing him in this silly song
the guy was wrong

Looks like this guy didn't care
we just run like we're scared
he didn't care

The guy won't care
looks like he never will
oh, well

If you're outside the box, you're inside the circle
Seeing the green, & keeping it purple
You're outside the box, you know you're for real
So, Dance like you have to, dance like the devil.

Guy Stickney

A PUPPY DOG TALE

Once upon a time there was an old dog on a farm named Lucy. Lucy was a gift to her friend Gus on his fifth birthday. The minute they met each other, they knew they'd be friends.

One day Dad said, "Hi Gus, it's almost your birthday. Do you want to go up north and pick out a puppy? There's some farmers up north who have a litter of Border Collies."

"Sure," said Gus. It sounded great to him, and off they went.

When they got to the other farmer's place way up north, there was a litter of five or six puppies left. Gus picked out the one he wanted, and Dad paid them. Away they went.

On the way home, Dad asked Gus, "What do you want to name her?" Gus said, "Lucy," because he had seen on TV that the oldest humanoid skeleton so far discovered just happened to be named Lucy too.

All the way home, Gus kept Lucy on the floor of the truck. She was so nervous, she dribbled pee all over his leg. When they got home, Gus was happy.

Lucy was small and that made a perfect friend for Gus because he was small himself. At first Gus's mom had to feed Lucy puppy food because she was so little. Until she grew out of that, she remained inside most of the time. She liked to go under the staircase that led up to the living room from the kitchen. She would hide under there, even when she got old.

The poor puppy took a while to get house trained. Eventually, she learned not to pee on the floor.

One day, Gus (And his bad self) noticed that Lucy hadn't messed up the newspaper underneath the stairs. Gus (of course) was the only one small enough to get under there. So, he went under the stairs and peed all over the place. He was afraid of getting in trouble for that one but neither Mom nor Dad ever said anything.

On the farm where Gus lived, there were two dogs already. One was a Bull Terrier named Florence and the other was a Hungarian Kuvasz named Victor. Florence would eat anything except pickles. Victor was so big that when he stood next to Gus, they were eye to eye.

One day, Lucy and Gus were out in the yard and looking around the horse's water pails. They came up to one pail and Gus looked inside. There was a bee drowning in the water. Gus saw this and a little voice on his shoulder asked him, "Do you care enough to save this bee from this pail of water?" When Gus heard this, he put his hands together and splashed the bee out of the pail and onto the ground. He didn't bring it back and show Mom because he didn't want to get stung. So, he let it get its breath back and fly away on its own.

The next day, Gus and Lucy were in the yard and at the exact same time, they both saw a magpie out on the lawn. They both stopped dead in their tracks "Get em Lucy." At that moment, Lucy ran after the magpie, tackled it, and killed it. As if saving the bee from the pail of water enabled Lucy and Gus the ability to kill the magpie, which Lucy later ate.

The dogs were always starved on the farm because my dad didn't have a lot of money and the nearest Safeway was 39 mi away. Later, Dad drowned most of the puppies from a litter. The ones he couldn't use or couldn't sell. Too many mouths, Gus himself was lucky he could read and write.

One night, about 10:00 PM Mom let Florence out to pee and Florence never came back. Mom couldn't believe it. Dad thought one of the neighbors had shot her. The next day, Dad and Gus drove all around looking for Florence's tracks in the snow. When they finally found what looked like her tracks, they followed them in the red truck and eventually, the tracks led into a thicket. They decided not to follow any further because it was someone else's land. Florence was old and when everybody got home, they decided that it was her time to go, and she knew. So, she went somewhere where she could go to die.

Dad had to replace Florence with another Bull Terrier. So, we drove way into the city and Dad got an older male Bull Terrier named Cromb.

Cromb was the dumbest dog ever. He would go to sleep under the wheels of the truck and get run over. That didn't even stop him. He also got Lucy pregnant. Dad was asking two hundred-fifty bucks for the puppies. Apparently, they were a good cross.

The next time she had puppies, it was because of an old German Shepherd that came into the yard while she was in heat. "I hate German Shepherds," Thought Gus. And of course, they had more puppies.

Now, Gus was six in Grade one. He was starting to learn the ropes in school and having a good time. He was happy in school and even though the other kids laughed at him a lot, he was fine. Sometimes the girls who were working on the farm at that time would take him out to lunch. He really enjoyed that.

One day Kim, who was one of the hands, got fired by Gus's mom. Gus used to always help the hands clean the stalls. When Gus went to help that day Kim was upset and she just shook him and said, "What's wrong with you?" Gus didn't know why Kim never came back.

Gus had made some friends in school. Besides the ones that laughed at him at first, there were some good ones.

One day Gus's mom came up to him and said, "I've been thinking about this for a long time and we're gonna leave your father. Gus said, "What about my friends?" Mom said he would make new friends. He never really did though.

Mom said they were gonna stay with Gus's aunt and then move down to Grandma & GP's house. The first trip down, Mom took Kit who was Gus's little brother first and then came back for Gus.

When they made the second trip down to the states, Mom got two cassette tapes. Even though the car didn't have a tape player, Mom got a boom box. Mom got the Beatles and The Beach Boys. Gus liked one Beatles song and some of the Beach Boys. Kit liked the Beach Boys the most. He loves Hawiian pizza too.

When they got to the border, they were held up for five hours. The cops had to search the entire vehicle and then told them the car was designed for a

Canadian, but they would let them go anyway. So, they made it to Grandma and GP's.

Grandma and GP lived on a small island in the San Juans. Gus was now forced to go to school on Shaw and live with his grandparents while Kit and Mom moved to Lopez. Mom got a job.

GP taught Gus all about what it was like to be homeless. He made Gus sleep on the couch in his clothes with a sleeping bag. Gus borrowed a bike to get to school and back on his own. The only help he needed was getting up Airport Hill every morning. GP would give him a lift.

Then it became Christmas and Gus's school wrote a play. The play was followed by a talent show. Gus's part in the play was to play the homeless kid. He had to dig potatoes out of a garbage can and his only lines were, "One potato, two potato, three potato."

In the talent show, Gus sang part of a song about Brian Mulrooney and another song he wrote himself about Kit.

During the Christmas holiday, Gus moved to Lopez to be with his mom and brother. Mom found a boyfriend. His name was Joe. Joe was rich and he bought Gus and Kit a Nintendo for Christmas.

Gus started school on Lopez now and had a crabby teacher. She had given all her students pencils with their names on them already, but Gus didn't get one because he was new. Gus begged and she ordered some for him after he coaxed her into doing it. She was unhappy about it too. The pencils sucked & got grinded up in the pencil sharpener all at once.

Everything was going fine until a kid who had been gone moved back. He had seniority over Gus who rode the same bus. So, the bus driver came up to Gus and said, "So and so has moved back, and I have to change the bus route. So, now you have to walk a quarter mile home after school from the bus stop." "Bummer ain't it." No sympathy!

One day in school, the teacher showed them Haley's Comet was passing by Earth. They all went outside, and they could see it with their own eyes.

Right after that, the news said Arctic air was blowing in from Alaska and we were gonna have a bad storm. The teacher sent them all home to get ready for the storm.

When Gus and Kit woke up the next morning, it was 20 degrees below zero in the house and Mom was frantic because trees had fallen on some of the cows. One of the walls blew in too. So, the house was very cold. It wasn't even their house. They were allowed to stay there as long as they fed the cows. Mom was scared running around, trying to save cows. After it was all over, they ended up with an orphaned calf. They named him Buddy and bottle fed him, but he eventually died.

The old barflies said they'd never have a storm like that again for 30 years. Then it happened again. It wasn't quite as cold as the first one, but Gus was used to the cold. He was Canadian. After the second storm there was another orphaned calf, but he died too.

Well, Summer came along, and Gus's mom was told if they stayed another year, they would have to pay rent. Mom was not happy after all they had been through. They moved to the mainland to a town called Mount Hermon and Gus began third grade.

One day, Gus looked at a penny and it said "1989". Gus thought, "it's amazing how far we've gotten. It's already 1989".

Every summer, Kit and Gus flew up to their dads and spent a few weeks with him. That was all dad got.

They had BBQ's and worked in the fields. When Gus was 12, he learned how to drive a tractor and a truck with a manual transmission. You're supposed to pop the clutch in the truck & ride the clutch on the tractor, but Gus had a hard time understanding that. He did the opposite and took a lot of heat for it too.

Once they had all the hay baled at the end of summer, Dad put the tractor in fifth gear (top speed fifteen mph) and told Gus to drive it back to the yard and park it in front of the fuel tanks. This was the moment of truth because there was a difficult turn off the road into the driveway. Either the tractor goes in the ditch, the baler goes in the ditch, or you make it. Gus Made it. He didn't park close enough to the fuel tank. He hoped his dad understood.

When mom left, something happened to Cromb. Gus didn't know but Cromb was a city dog and not wise. Dad got a third Bull Terrier and named her Florence the second. She was Kit's dog.

Lucy had puppies. Quite a few litters. We're not sure how many. At one time Dad had a German Shepherd Rottweiler cross named Ricky. He was a good dog and never begged at their BBQ's. Ricky and Lucy had puppies and Florence chewed one of the puppies up when it was still little. The dog grew into Badger. Badger was a great dog. He would never come up to you or anybody. The only time they ever petted him was during thunderstorms. Then he was tame and would come inside. Probably because of being attacked.

Once, Gus went to Canada to visit Dad without Kit. Gus was 19 and he had been in some trouble. When he got to the farm, there were two puppies under the deck. It was a litter of five, but Dad had drowned the three girls before Gus got there. There were two pups left. Panda and Ratty. Panda was Gus's right away.

One day, they went to the city so Dad could do horse business and when they came home, Panda ran out and told them there were dead chickens. It was Ratty and his mother Dixie who had killed chickens.

First, they took Ratty and threw him in an old laundry basket with a bunch of rocks. Then taped him inside and threw him in the dugout. A dugout is a small man-made pond. Then they tried to do the same with Dixie, but she got out. So, then they just taped her paws and mouth. The hired hand did her in, Gus couldn't go.

Now, by this time, Lucy was fourteen years old and when Gus got there at first, she was hobbling around, and she had a cyst on the side of her body. The puppies wanted to play, and Lucy kept them busy, but she was dying.

One day some people brought a mare to Gus's dad so his dad could breed the mare. The mare wouldn't start horsing so they had to call the vet to bring a shot. Gus's dad asked them to bring a shot to put Lucy down too. When the vet got there, she didn't have the shot for the dog, just the horse.

Gus took them into the yard and showed them why he wanted to put his dog down. Lucy was laying in the driveway and barely breathing. The vet's husband started yelling at Gus, "Step on her neck, she's suffering!" etc. Gus just picked her up and put her in the barn.

The next day, Gus dug a hole in the lawn and Dad pulled a rock over her grave next to the grave of his dog Jumbo and that's the end.

Goosepunk

Guy Stickney

CERTAIN DEATH

It appears to me things aren't how they seem and
the evil in the air isn't going anywhere It appears
as well that the sensitive smell Wasn't coming up
indeed, it was coming from thee Now, healthy as it
seems
We are not into god
Take it from the best probably isn't nothing left
Welcome to the end, the beginning my friend
As it now appears to be
Certain Death un-wish I see

ABOUT THE AUTHOR

My name is Author Guy Stickney. I write under the name Goosepunk. I got the name from an old punk song off the Descendents album "Cool to be You." The genre I write in is a lowered rant like the language of punk. You can find my books at Xlibris.com, Amazon.com & Barnes & Noble's bookstores. I call my studio, Alienated Studios, or just plain Guy's Room Studios. Nothing's set in stone. You can get a hold of me at guystickney2@gmail.com.

ACKNOWLEDGEMENT

We owe a debt of gratitude to the authors who submitted their work to this endeavor. To contest editors Robert Mottram and Naomi Wark. To contest judges Rick Clark, William Kenower, and Mary Trimble. To Melba Burke for the book layout and design. To Clark Graham for the eBook conversion. And Joseph Vitovec for the cover photograph of Skagit River, and Rebaca Covers for the cover design.

88321169R00134